LORD ROBERTS
OF KANDAHAR, V.C

The Life-Story of a Great Soldier

BY

WALTER JERROLD

AUTHOR OF "SIR REDVERS H. BULLER, V.C.: THE STORY
OF HIS LIFE AND CAMPAIGNS," ETC., ETC.

WITH NINE ILLUSTRATIONS

London

S. W. PARTRIDGE & CO.

8 AND 9, PATERNOSTER ROW

1900

PREFACE

IN 1881 a public speaker referred to Sir Frederick Roberts, as he then was, as the most popular man in England, and there was no exaggeration in the statement. The fame of the great soldier's triumphant march from Kabul to Kandahar was, of course, then fresh in men's minds. To-day, when the story of that march is nearly twenty years old, it has come to be the lot of the man who was its dominating spirit to enter, at an age when he might excusably have been looking towards the quietude of retirement, upon such a task as has not fallen to any other military leader of our time. The task which Lord Roberts has undertaken in South Africa is likely to make many readers wish for some slight outline sketch of his career, that they may have, in brief compass, the record of the achievements which won for, and maintain Lord Roberts in, the position of one of the most popular men of his time. Such outline is all this small book pretends to be.

Lord Roberts has himself, in his fascinating volume, "Forty-one Years in India," given us

a book which not only deserves to rank with
the classics of autobiography, but also to be
accorded a place among the most valuable of
the historical works concerned with the growth
of the British Empire in India. The success
achieved by that book was instant and well-
deserved, and it may be hoped that some
readers of this small volume will have their
interest in the great soldier stimulated so that
they may determine to read, in his own words,
the detailed record of his long and valued
service in India, and the history of the India
in which he served.

As Commander-in-Chief of the British forces
in South Africa, Field-Marshal Lord Roberts
has the eyes of the world on his every action
towards reinstating the British prestige where
it has within the past few months been so
rudely shaken. After the disaster to our arms
at Maiwand he it was who saved the situation
by his great victory at Kandahar. That the
same good generalship may give us the same
result in South Africa is the sincere hope of
the many thousands of his countrymen and
women whom he has taught to have implicit
confidence in his bravery and in his military
genius. This compilation of the story of his
life will at least show that the country has
every reason for having that implicit confidence in the generalship and judgment of the
hero of Kandahar.

CONTENTS

LIST OF ILLUSTRATIONS

LORD ROBERTS OF KANDAHAR, V.C.:

The Life-Story of a Great Soldier

CHAPTER I

A soldier-son of a soldier—Born in India—Sir Abraham Roberts' career—Lord Roberts' education—His first commission.

FIELD - MARSHAL Lord Roberts of Kandahar and Waterford is at once one of the greatest and one of the most popular soldiers of the time. Up to within the past few weeks his distinguished services have for the most part been given in India, but now when he is gone to gain, as we all sincerely hope, fresh laurels in South Africa,

it cannot but be interesting to go over the
story of his career. The great soldier is
himself the son of a distinguished military
officer, who earned the gratitude of his
country for his services in connection with
the building up and consolidating of the
British Empire in the East.

Frederick Sleigh Roberts was born in India,
at Cawnpore, on September 30, 1832. But
though born in India he is, as he has again
and again insisted upon in the days of his
success, an Irishman. The country which
gave to the British Empire its greatest military
leader of the beginning of the nineteenth century in Arthur Wellesley, Duke of Wellington,
also gave the greatest soldier to the end of the
same century in the person of Frederick Sleigh
Roberts. By both sides of his family the soldier
is Irish, with a slight dash of French Huguenot
blood from one of his maternal ancestors. In
1712 there was born a John Roberts, who
won some fame for himself as an architect in
the city of Waterford. Present inhabitants of
that city are familiar with some of his work,
for he is known to have designed the Town

Hall, the Cathedral Catholic Chapel, and the Leper Hospital. This John Roberts married Mary Susannah Sautelle, a lady of French extraction and daughter of Major Sautelle who served in King William the Third's footguards at the Boyne, and who had settled at Waterford at the close of the seventeenth century. The architect lived to a ripe old age, dying in 1796; one of his sons, another John, became the grandfather of Lord Roberts, while two other sons were of some repute in their day as landscape painters. The second John Roberts became a clergyman and married the daughter of a Dublin clergyman whose family had long been connected with Waterford.

The third son of the Rev. John Roberts was named Abraham, and was born at Waterford on April 11, 1784. At the age of seventeen, in the first year of the present century, he was appointed to the Waterford regiment of militia, and a couple of years later became an Ensign in the 48th regiment. In 1804 he joined the service of the East India Company—a service which was then full of promise to an adventurous-minded youth. A year later he was promoted to the rank of Lieutenant and served with distinction in the Sutlej under Lord Lake. The next step in Abraham Roberts' promotion did not come until 1818, when he was made Captain, but meanwhile he had seen a good deal of varied service, and in 1814–15 served with considerable distinction under the command of Sir William Richards. In December of the earlier year, for example, he commanded his regiment at Birla Ke Tebee, and was actively engaged for the whole day close to the Fort of Istuk, where his courage was rewarded, for he finally succeeded in capturing the Indian chieftain to whom he was opposed and completely routed the enemy's force. In 1826 he received further promotion, being gazetted a Major, and two years later was presented by the Governor-General of India (Lord Amherst) with a piece of plate in recognition of valuable departmental services.

In 1830 Major Roberts married his second wife, Isabella, widow of Major Maxwell, and daughter of Major Abraham Bunbury of the 62nd Foot, and of Kilfeacle, county Tipperary.

In 1832—the year which saw the birth of his more illustrious son—Abraham Roberts became Lieutenant-Colonel. In 1838 he was given command of a Brigade in the first Afghan War, and was present at the storming and capture of Ghuznee. In 1840 he took command of Shah Shuja's forces, but did not retain it for long, resigning and returning to the service of the East India Company because the precautions which he wisely advised were not adopted. He foresaw the danger at Kabul, and had his advice been taken the subsequent disasters might have been averted. Shah Shuja, it may be said, was the candidate for the Kabul throne who had secured British support, and whose ambition cost him his life. In 1843 Roberts *père* became a full colonel. From 1852 to the close of 1853 he was in command of the Peshawar division, in which position his exercise of judgment and calm observation obtained the grateful acknowledgment of the Government of India. In the autumn of 1853 his health was such that he

was compelled to bring his half century of
sterling service in India to a close, but it must
have been especially gratifying to the veteran
to know that he was leaving behind him a very
promising officer in the person of his young
son.   Before taking up the story of that son's
career it may be as well to finish this outline sketch of that of his father.   The year
after leaving India he became a Major-General,
and in 1857 a Lieutenant-General, the full
rank of General following in 1864.   In 1865
he was made a K.C.B., and on December 8,
1873, he was invested with the insignia of a
G.C.B.   A few days later he was taken ill,
and on December 28th he died at Clifton,
having nearly completed his ninetieth year.

Frederick Sleigh Roberts, the illustrious son
of a distinguished father, was born, then, at
Cawnpore on September 30, 1832.   While
still a baby his parents brought him to
England in 1834, his father having a couple
of years' leave.   When his parents returned to
India in 1836 they left the child to be brought
up and educated in England, the climate of
India rendering it necessary that the children

of European parents should pass their tenderer years in more equable latitudes. In those mid-years of the nineteenth century an officer on Indian service got but rare opportunities of visiting his native land, so that young Roberts saw his father but little before he went out and joined him as a soldier. In 1844 the elder Roberts returned home on leave, and his son was then a schoolboy, dreaming already it may be imagined of following in that father's footsteps. His childhood was passed at Clifton, where he began his education with a couple o years (1838–1840) at a dame's school. Later he was for another couple of years with a French schoolmaster at Clifton, and from 1842 to 1845 was pupil of a Mr. Mills at Hampton. In the autumn of the last-mentioned year he was entered at Eton— training-ground of many great soldiers, of whom I may appropriately cite Lord Roberts' present companion in arms in South Africa, Sir Redvers Buller. Young Roberts was placed in the Fourth Form at Eton, but did not remain very long at the great educational foundation near Windsor, for he left it in July,

2

1846, and some months later was entered at
Sandhurst. At Eton it is worth noting that
he had among his schoolfellows (the future
Sir) Alfred Lyall, who was destined to make
for himself a brilliant reputation, and whom his
whilom school companion met again during
one of the most remarkable events of the
Indian Mutiny.

It was in January, 1847, that young
Roberts, with his mind now definitely set
upon a military career, was entered a pupil
at the military training college at Sandhurst.
There he remained for some eighteen months,
and "took three out of the six steps required
for a commission without purchase." At Sandhurst his school honours included a prize for
German. A friend of Roberts' father then
secured for the military student a presentation
to Addiscombe, the special training centre for
soldiers taking service under the East India
Company. It was some time before a vacancy
occurred, and Roberts did not actually begin
his studentship at Addiscombe until February,
1850. Towards the close of the following year
he entered for the final examination, the

passing of which qualified him for a commission. Despite the fact that his health during the period of work at Addiscombe had been but indifferent, when the list of successful candidates was published, he was found to be the ninth out of about four dozen. The result of his success was that, on December 12th, he was duly appointed Second Lieutenant in the Bengal Artillery.

CHAPTER II

Eastward bound—At Dum-Dum—A long journey—Aide-de-Camp to his father—Life at Peshawar—Sir Abraham's retirement—Joining the Horse Artillery —The eve of the Mutiny.

"FROM the time of Clive up to the present day," wrote the subject of this biography a few years ago, "India has been a valuable training school for the British army." It was a school in which he himself learned many lessons and won many honours during four decades. It was in February, 1852, when he was but a few months past completing his nineteenth year, that Frederick Roberts set out on his first long journey to the East—a journey which was destined to be significant of much not only in the life-story of the soldier himself, but in the history of his country. It is true, as we saw in the last chapter, that the future Commander-in-Chief of the forces in India was born in that land, but he had left it as an infant, and was returning to it as to an unknown field in which, as a man, he was to do his best in following in the footsteps of a distinguished father and in carving out for himself a career. India, then, really represented to the young cadet much that is most significant in the word home—it was his birthplace, and it was there that his father was then holding an honourable command after half a century spent in the military service of the growing Indian Empire. Nearly fifty years have elapsed since young Roberts journeyed to take up his first duties in the East, and that period has seen vast changes in the circumstances attending a journey to the Orient. Then the steamboat service was vastly inferior to that of the present, then there was no Suez Canal to draw more closely together the East and the West, and passengers had to leave the mail steamers at Alexandria, get thence to Cairo by canal boats and Nile steamers, and from

Cairo to Suez had to proceed over about ninety miles of desert "in a conveyance closely resembling a bathing machine." From Suez fresh mail steamers conveyed passengers to the various Oriental ports. The heat during the journey through the Red Sea was terribly great, and young Roberts is reported to have said, "I don't know how we shall fight in India if it is as hot as this!" Having set out from Southampton on February 20th, Cadet Roberts reached his destination, Calcutta, on April 1st.

Supernumerary Second Lieutenant Roberts —for such was his official designation at the time—was appointed to a native field battery, and proceeded to Dum-Dum (about eight miles north-east of Calcutta) to take up his duties. Dum-Dum, which had at one time been an important military centre of the East India Company's service, though in the early 'fifties the garrison was much reduced, was, however, then the headquarters of the Artillery to which the young aspirant for military honours had been posted, and it was there that he passed the first few months of his

long Indian career. The town of Dum-Dum*
is situated (to use the words of the Indian
Gazetteer compiled by Mr. Edward Thornton
in 1854) in the British district called the
Twenty-four Pergunnahs, and was formerly
the headquarters of artillery for the presidency
of Bengal. Between Lieutenant Roberts'
arrival and the compilation of the *Gazetteer*
that headquarters was removed to Meerut.
"In the vicinity of Dum-Dum" (to continue
Mr. Thornton's summary) "is the cannon
foundry, of which a military writer thus
speaks: 'This cannon foundry is in every
respect better contrived than that of Wool-
wich. It contains a boring-room in which
twelve brass guns may be bored at the same
time, for the Government procures the iron
guns from Europe. During the time I was
there six guns were cast, and the arrangements are such that three times the number
might have been manufactured.'"

Roberts was only at the Artillery head-

* To-day the name of the place is familiar to every
one who reads the daily papers as having become that of
one of the deadliest of the bullets used in modern warfare.

quarters for about four months, but it was long enough for a feeling of home-sickness to grow upon the young officer. It was, of course, comparatively solitary for one who had been so recently in the college at Addiscombe and then for some weeks with his friends and fellow-travellers on the journey out. It is probable that most young soldiers feel that as soon as they join the army they want to see active service, and it is by no means surprising to find that Lieutenant Roberts looked forward to an opportunity of joining the Burma expedition then preparing, as a welcome change from the "slow" life at Dum-Dum.

The slowness of that life was somewhat diversified in an alarming fashion when the neighbourhood was visited by a terrific cyclone. Roberts had been dining with a friend about half a mile away from his own bungalow, when an ever-rising wind gave warning of the impending storm. He left his friend's early, attended by a native servant carrying a lantern. They had not proceeded far before a gust of wind blew out the light, and the servant went on, thinking apparently that the officer was following him : " I shouted to him as loudly as I could, but the uproar was so terrific that he could not hear a word, and there was nothing for it but to try and make my own way home. The darkness was profound. As I was walking carefully along I suddenly came in contact with an object, which a timely flash of lightning showed me was a column, standing in exactly the opposite direction from my own house. I could now locate myself correctly, and the lightning becoming every moment more vivid, I was enabled to grope my way by slow degrees to the mess, where I expected to find someone to show me my way home, but the servants, who knew from experience the probable effects of a cyclone, had already closed the outside Venetian shutters and barred all the doors. I could just see them through the crack engaged in making everything fast. In vain I banged at the door and called at the top of my voice—they heard nothing. Reluctantly I became convinced that there was no alternative but to leave my shelter and face the rapidly increasing storm once more. My bungalow was not more than half a mile away, but it took me an age to accomplish this short distance, as I was only able to move a few steps at a time, whenever the lightning showed me the way. It was necessary to be careful, as the road was raised, with a deep ditch on either side; several trees had already been blown down and lay across it, and huge branches were being driven through the air like thistle-down. I found extreme difficulty in keeping my feet, especially at the cross-roads, where I was more than once all but blown over. At last I reached my house, but even then my struggles were not quite at an end. It was a very long time before I could gain admittance. The servant who had been carrying the lantern had arrived, and, missing me, imagined that I must have returned to the house at which I had dined. The men with whom I chummed, thinking it unlikely that I should make a second attempt to return home, had carefully fastened all the doors, momentarily expecting the roof of the house to be blown off. I had to continue hammering for a long time before they heard and admitted me, thankful to be comparatively safe inside a house." *

Next day, "Dum-Dum in ruins was even more dreary than before," the whole place looking as if it had suffered a severe bombardment. The cyclone was an exciting incident in a life of somewhat dull routine, and Lieutenant Roberts thought he would try and get a change, so he wrote to his father, inquiring if he could not get him sent to Burma. The veteran officer replied to his eager son that he was hoping to be shortly given the command of the Peshawar division —the largest and most important in India— and that they should then be together.

The change was not long in coming about. It was early in April that Roberts reached Calcutta; in August he bid farewell to Dum-Dum and set out on the formidable journey to join his father at Peshawar. Long and tedious that journey must have been in those pre-railway days. With brief stoppages by the way the

* Lord Roberts' "Forty-One Years in India" (Macmillan & Co.).

Lieutenant took close upon three months to
get from Calcutta to Peshawar, arriving there
at the beginning of November. He rested for
a few days at his birthplace, Cawnpore, and at
Meerut met for the first time a body of the
famous Bengal Horse Artillery, with the result
that he formed a "fixed resolve to leave no
stone unturned in the endeavour to become a
horse-gunner."

Association with his father at the time was
no doubt simply invaluable to the development
of the future Field-Marshal. Major-General
Roberts, who was then in his sixty-ninth year,
had seen much of Afghan warfare in the troubles
of a decade or so earlier, and his knowledge
and advice must have stood his son in good
stead when, a quarter of a century later, he
was performing his notable services in the
same part of Asia. Lieutenant Roberts lived
with his father and acted as his aide-de-camp,
though he also continued doing his duties as
officer with the 2nd Company 2nd Battalion
of the Bengal Artillery (known locally as
"The Devil's Own").

It was not for very long that Frederick

Roberts was to be with his father at Peshawar, for before he had been there a year the elder officer's health began to give way, and he had consequently to relinquish his command. The doctor ordered him to return to England before the winter set in, and so, towards the end of November, 1853, he set out on his long journey to the coast, accompanied by his son, who intended taking him as far as Rawal Pindi. Young Roberts only went with his father for a couple of days on his way, as the invalid improved so much by the change that it was no longer necessary. Those two days, however, sufficed to make him miss, much to his regret, a first chance of fighting, for the Mountain Battery into which his company had been converted, and of which he was the only subaltern, had been ordered off on an expedition against some Afridi villages. The eager lieutenant hurried back, but though he got within sound of the firing, it was all over by the time that he reached his battery.

Two notable incidents of his early Peshawar experiences stamped themselves on his memory. One was the having to witness a " barbarous

and degrading" flogging parade, and the other
was a comforting example for the superstitious.
"On the 1st January, 1853, thirteen of us
dined together; eleven years after we were all
alive, nearly the whole of the party having
taken part in the suppression of the Mutiny,
and five or six having been wounded."

The veteran soldier had been invalided
home, but the young artillery officer passed
by no means unscathed through the trying
climate of India. During the winter of 1853–
54 he suffered much from fever, so much so
that in the following April he was granted six
months' leave of absence that he might visit
a more equable climate, and he went off for a
journey through the far-famed vale of Kashmir.
The young subalterns, for Roberts was accompanied by a lieutenant of the Horse Artillery
must have had a magnificent holiday, travelling
amid some of the grandest and some of the
most beautiful scenery which the world has to
show. After an enjoyable and health-im-
proving holiday Lieutenant Roberts returned
to his duties at Peshawar, and shortly after
received the coveted "jacket" of a lieutenant

in the Bengal Horse Artillery, a force which Colonel Malleson has described as "unsurpassed and unsurpassable"—the force which he had wished to join from the moment when he fell in with a body of it on his first journey to Peshawar a couple of years earlier.

The troop to which he was posted was the first of the 2nd Brigade of Bengal Horse Artillery—a troop which was composed for the most part of a fine body of men, nearly all of them Irishmen, most of whom, as their new lieutenant remarked, could have lifted him with one hand. Again when winter came the officer was more or less severely prostrated by fever, and early in 1855 he was granted eight months' leave of absence in accordance with a medical certificate, and set off once again on a travel in search of renewed health. The condition attached to his leave was that he should at the expiration of the eight months report himself at Mian Mir, there to undergo the course of riding instruction rendered necessary by his new position. Again he selected Kashmir as the country in which to pass the first part of his holiday,

and again he found congenial company for
the long trip. He remained in the country
celebrated in song until August, and then
set out on a four hundred miles' march
across the great Himalayan range of mountains to Simla.

The visit to Simla proved the "turning-
point" in the officer's career. While at that
now widely famous centre, but which was
then a comparatively unimportant place, Lieutenant Roberts had the good fortune to lunch
with the Quartermaster-General (Colonel
Becher), who in the course of conversation
expressed a desire to have his companion,
when an opportunity occurred, attached to
his department. This was of course very
gratifying, for Roberts was, as might be
imagined, an ambitious soldier, and fully
recognised the great value of a staff appointment to any one who aspired to the exercise of important powers. His opportunity
came—as opportunities generally do—with
unexpected suddenness, and much sooner
than he would have dared to anticipate.
Early in 1856 the Deputy-Assistant-Quarter-

master-General was required for special
service, and Lieutenant Roberts was offered
the post during his absence on condition
that he "doubled the parts," and did his
regimental work as well as that pertaining
to the staff appointment. This of course
he readily agreed to. His high hopes were,
however, soon dashed, for the Governor-
General refused to sanction his occupation
of the post because he had not passed the
necessary examination in Hindustani. This
was in May, and Roberts promptly resolved
to qualify. He set to work with such good
will and such zealous application that when
examination-time came round in July he
was able to pass the requisite test. Shortly
afterwards his labour met with its reward,
and he was appointed temporary occupant
of the coveted post, thus getting his foot on
the first rung of the ladder of staff-promotion.

The autumn of 1856 proved a bad one for
the troops at Peshawar, and a camp was
formed away from the headquarters for the
benefit of the soldiers' health. In October a
special practice camp for the artillery was

3

arranged for a couple of months at a spot
five miles from Peshawar, and when there
Lieutenant Roberts experienced something
of the difficulty of reconciling his duties as
D.A.Q.M.G. with his work as an officer of
the artillery. Before the practice camp was
broken up he had to join the Divisional-
General (Reed), who was on his tour of
inspection at Rawal Pindi, and that he might
stay up to the last moment with his troop
he left but one day in which to do a horseback journey of a hundred miles. He
managed, with but one short rest for necessary refreshment, to get over the ground in
eleven hours ! Shortly before Christmas his
temporary occupation of the D.A.Q.M.G.'s
position came to an end on the return of
the regular official.

On the first day of the new year—that year
fraught with such terrible significance in the
history of our Empire in the East—Roberts
was present at a remarkable meeting which took
place at the Khyber Pass between Sir John
Lawrence (then Chief Commissioner of the
Punjab) and the Amir of Afghanistan. Early

in 1857 Roberts was gratified by being once
again selected to occupy the position of
D.A.Q.M.G. during the absence of that
officer. Again he had to accompany General
Reed on his tour of inspection, and when at
Rawal Pindi received a flattering offer the
acceptance of which would have altered the
whole tenor of his career and robbed the
British army of one of its greatest commanders. There he once more met the Chief
Commissioner, and Sir John Lawrence then
offered him an appointment in the Public
Works Department. Tempting as this might
have been from a monetary point of view,
the young soldier was too strongly attached
to his chosen profession to wish to change,
and he therefore declined. The early spring
passed thus in a tour of inspection and in
the ordinary routine of regimental and official
duties. When carrying on his work as
D.A.Q.M.G. he was ordered to report on
Cherat as a sanatorium, and while surveying
the district fell in with the Deputy-Com-
missioner of the Punjab, then on his tour of
inspection. This was none other than the

famous John Nicholson—one of the greatest
of the many great men whose powers have
been called into action in India, a man who
though he was killed in action before Delhi at
the early age of thirty-five had yet impressed
European and native alike with a sense of
the greatness and nobility of his character.
Indeed we are told that among some of the
frontier tribes he was looked up to as to a
god—loved as much as feared—was actually
worshipped by some of them, who formed
themselves into a sect, taking his name as
their distinctive title.

On returning to Peshawar at the end of April
Roberts anticipated having a long round of
regular routine, but the opening tragedies of
the great Indian Mutiny were very few days
ahead, and before long he was to be in "the
very thick of it" in that great struggle when
British supremacy in the East was on its
trial. The Mutiny did not come without
warning, but the premonitory symptoms of
trouble did not suggest to those on the spot
anything of its possible extent. For months
"throughout the length and breadth of India

there was distress, revolt, bloodshed, and bitter distrust of our native troops."

One thing that is known—although there are by no means wanting historians who deny its association with the Mutiny—is that for some time before there had been a mysterious distribution to the natives, far and wide, of "chupattees," little unleavened cakes made of coarse flour—a distribution which is said to have preceded a local mutiny at the close of the eighteenth century, and which is also said to have been utilised by the superstitious as a means of warding off disease.

In the book written on the Indian Mutiny by the Rev. J. Cave-Brown, who became Chaplain of the Punjab Movable Column, we are told that: "One district officer, who saw a chupattee-laden messenger arrive in a village, and observed him breaking his cake into pieces and distributing them among the men of the village, asked what it meant; he was told that there was an old custom in Hindustan that when their *malik*, or chief, required any service from his people, he adopted this mode to prepare them for receiving his orders, and everyone who partook of this chupattee was held 'pledged to obey the order, whenever it might come and whatever it might be.' 'What was the nature of the order in the present case?' he asked; the answer, accompanied by a suspicious smile, was, 'We don't know yet.'"

Lord Roberts himself, it is interesting to note, seems to associate the distribution of the "chupattees" with the subsequent troubles, in which, as we shall see, he bore his part like a true hero.

CHAPTER III

Outbreak of the Mutiny—Joins the Movable Column—
Drastic measures—Bound for the front—The Ridge
before Delhi—Assault and capture of the city.

OF all the " times that tried men's souls "
within the memory of people yet living,
there was none more terrible than that of the
Indian Mutiny—a trial which nearly cost us
our Empire in the East, but which in the
long run can be seen to have had a consolidating effect. When the Mutiny commenced
British India was still under the control of the
East India Company; when the Mutiny was
finally stamped out the vast tract of country
had become a dependency of the British
Crown, and that era of progress was inau-
gurated which twenty years later was to result
in the assumption by her Majesty the Queen

of England of the supplementary title of
Empress of India. The Mutiny with its long
tale of suffering and heroism forms one of the
most lurid chapters of nineteenth century
history—a chapter various parts of which have
been written and re-written many times by
people who lived through its awful months,
and the complete chronicle of which fills many
volumes. It is not my intention here to
attempt any recapitulation of the incidents
of the Mutiny except in so far as they
were incidents in which the subject of this
biographical sketch was directly concerned.
Lord Roberts has himself told the story of the
Mutiny in his "Forty-one Years in India"
with a fulness of detail, a vividness of presentation, and a grasp of facts which leave
nothing to be desired; that story occupies,
indeed, rather more than a third of the
bulky volume in which he has given the fine
record of his whole forty-one years of service
in the East.

The broad facts of the Mutiny must be
taken as being familiar to my reader, for as
I have said I am concerned with it only in
so far as it affected, or was affected by,

Frederick Roberts. We have always been taught that the means employed by fanatics to bring about the native uprising against the European troops and residents in India were the dissemination of a statement that new cartridges which had been recently introduced were greased with a mixture of cow's-fat and lard—the former the product of a beast sacred to all Hindoos, and the latter the product of an animal taboo as "unclean" by all of Mohammedan faith. It was said that we aimed at destroying the "caste" of the native troops. Despite the denials by British officers, the belief spread with great rapidity and with disastrous results. What is really appalling to contemplate now is the fact that the supposed fanatics were justified to a certain extent in their supposition—justified, that is, in believing us to be forcing them—for but a brief period, and owing to oversight—to use materials contrary to their religious scruples, but not in believing that it was part of an organised attempt on the part of the English to force the religion of the conquerors on the conquered.

Early in 1857 the first signs of the coming

storm might have been noticed here and there throughout India; such signs were, however, judged each by itself, and not as connected indications of coming trouble. The first serious indications came with shocking suddenness in the massacre of officers and other Europeans at Meerut and Delhi on May 11th. This made instant action necessary, and in some places native troops were promptly disarmed, but in all too many instances the English officers of native troops could not believe that the men who had served under them for many years would prove disloyal—and paid the penalty for this faith in their men with their lives. Lieutenant Roberts was at the time stationed at Peshawar, and when Brigadier Neville Chamberlain formed his Movable Column he appointed the young officer to his staff. Steps had to be taken rapidly to disarm native troops in which the slightest disaffection was suspected, and young Roberts was soon in the very thick of the preparations for arresting and, if possible, stamping out the trouble. With his commanding officer he left Peshawar for Rawal

Pindi, where he was for some time busily employed in the office of the Chief Commissioner (Sir John Lawrence), "drafting and copying confidential letters and telegrams." After a week at Rawal Pindi he and Chamberlain set out on a mail-cart with the object of joining the Movable Column at Waziribad. They reached their destination on May 27th, a day after the Column had arrived there, and proceeded thence to Lahore, where they arrived on the last day of the month, and whither they were followed by the Column a couple of days later.

At Lahore the young officer came first into immediate contact with the grim realities of the time. Native troops were of course accompanying the Movable Column ; and though they had given no signs of trouble, it was known that they might rise at any moment against their officers and desert with their arms to Delhi, then the chief centre of the mutineers' power. Chamberlain and the young artillery officer were living in a house close to where the native troops were camped. The spies employed to keep a close

watch on the suspected soldiers had instructions to rouse Lieutenant Roberts on the
slightest signs of suspicious conduct. On the
night of June 8th the long-feared information
came, and Roberts was awakened to hear the
definite and unwelcome news "that the 35th
Native Infantry intended to revolt at daybreak, and that some of them had already
loaded their muskets." Roberts at once
roused Chamberlain, and the Brigadier
immediately resolved upon prompt and
drastic measures. He ordered a "Drum-
head Court Martial," composed of native
officers, realising that the finding of such
a court must necessarily have a greater
moral effect than that of a court composed of Europeans. The prisoners tried
were two men who, on the regiment being
hurriedly ordered to fall in, were found
to have their muskets loaded ; they were
found guilty of mutiny and sentenced to
death. The sentence was ordered to be
carried out immediately, and the young officer
described the event as follows : " Chamberlain decided that they should be blown away

from guns in the presence of their own comrades, as being the most awe-inspiring means of carrying the sentence into effect. A parade was at once ordered. The troops were drawn up so as to form three sides of a square; on the fourth side were two guns. As the prisoners were being brought to the parade one of them asked me if they were going to be blown from the guns. I said 'Yes.' He made no further remark, and they both walked steadily until they reached the guns, to which they were bound, when one of them requested that some rupees he had on his person might be saved for his relations. The Brigadier answered: 'It is too late!' The word of command was given; the guns went off simultaneously, and the two mutineers were launched into eternity. It was a terrible sight, and one likely to haunt the beholder for many a long day; but that was what was intended. I carefully watched the sepoys' faces to see how it affected them. They were evidently startled at the swift retribution which had overtaken their guilty comrades, but looked more crestfallen than shocked or

horrified, and we soon learnt that their determination to mutiny and make the best of
their way to Delhi was in nowise changed
at the scene they had witnessed." *

Two days after this condign punishment
had been awarded to those who first gave
evidence of mutinous conduct in the Movable
Column that column left Lahore and reached
Umritsar, whence Chamberlain went to take
up his new duties on his appointment as
Adjutant-General of the army. He was
succeeded in the command of the Column,
much to our hero's delight, by John
Nicholson, Roberts remaining as staff officer.
The Column was kept on the move first
to Jullundur, where an incident occurred
which illustrated the strength of Nicholson's
character and shows us something of the man
for whom his young assistant had a passionate
admiration. A durbar, or council, had been
arranged at Jullundur for the officers and
principal men with the Raja Kapurthala's
troops, and after it was over one of the general
officers of the Kapurthala army, the senior in

* Lord Roberts' "Forty-one Years in India."

rank, was leaving the room when General Nicholson stepped in front of him and authoritatively waved him back, allowing the rest of the visitors to pass out. Nicholson then turned to Major Lake, the Commissioner, in whose house the durbar had been held, and said, "Do you see that General Mehtab Sing has his shoes on?" The host acknowledged that he had noticed it, but sought to excuse the visitor's act, for, as it is necessary to explain, no native, in native dress, ever enters a room with his shoes on unless he intends to be disrespectful. Nicholson, who recognised the significance of the matter, then sternly addressed the native officer in Hindustani: "There is no possible excuse for such an act of gross impertinence. Mehtab Sing knows perfectly well that he would not venture to step on his own father's carpet save barefooted, and he has only committed this breach of etiquette to-day because he thinks we are not in a position to resent the insult, and that he can treat us as he would not have dared to do a month ago." The native officer looked naturally somewhat abashed, but John Nichol-

son was not the man to let him off with a
mere scolding, and finished emphatically, " If
I were the last Englishman left in Jullundur
you should not come into my room with your
shoes on. I hope the Commissioner will
now allow me to order you to take your
shoes off and carry them out in your own
hands, so that your followers may witness
your discomfiture." In telling the story many
years later the young artillery officer, who had
been a close observer of the scene, added,
" Mehtab Sing, completely cowed, meekly did
as he was told." The incident was a useful
lesson, not only to the delinquent, but also to
any other of the Kapurthala people who might
be waiting the turn of events.

On June 24th Jullundur was left, and
Lieutenant Roberts with a district official
went on ahead to select a parade-ground on
which to disarm the 35th Native Infantry, the
loyalty of which Nicholson had had only too
good reason to suspect. The disarmament
was carried out with surprising suddenness
on the following morning. The officers with
the Column were hoping to receive orders to
continue the journey to Delhi, the siege of

which place was one of the greatest features
of the struggle between the mutineers and the
British forces, but instead, however, the Movable Column was ordered back to Umritsar,
much to our young hero's disappointment. He
was, not unnaturally, eager to be where the
struggle bid fair to be most severe. His
opportunity came sooner than he would have
dared to hope, for before the return to Umritsar had begun an urgent message was
received by General Nicholson asking that
all artillery officers not actually engaged on
their regimental duty might be sent to the
assistance of the Delhi force ; a message which
might have been penned for the obtaining of
the help of the young staff officer who was so
eager for his first fight.

The next morning saw Lieutenant Roberts
on a mail-cart hurrying forward, leaving his
servants to follow with his horses, etc., at the
earliest opportunity. He reached Delhi on
June 28th, and then heard details of the gallant
stand which the force had already made in
attacking the mutineers in their almost impregnable stronghold—the great city of the
Moghul Emperors. He was appointed Deputy-

Assistant-Quartermaster-General, and then, at his own request, was transferred to the same position with the artillery. For the next three months the story of his life is the story of the memorable Siege.

It was on the 10th of May that the flames of mutiny broke out at Meerut, whence the mutineers on the following day proceeded to Delhi, where they were joined by the native regiments there, and where British officers of native troops and all European inhabitants were ruthlessly murdered, the native soldiers either taking part in the murders, or at the least refusing to fire when ordered. Major H. E. S. Abbot, the senior of the half-dozen officers who survived the massacre, wrote a full report of the events, in the course of which he said: "From all I could glean there is not the slightest doubt that this insurrection has been originated and matured in the palace of the King of Delhi, and that with his full knowledge and sanction in the mad attempt to establish himself in the sovereignty of this country. It is well known that he has called on the neighbouring States to co-operate with him in thus trying to subvert the existing Government. The method he adopted appears to be to have gained the sympathy of the 38th Regiment Light Infantry by spreading the lying reports now going through the country of the Government having it in contemplation to upset their religion and have them all forcibly inducted to Christianity."

The mutineers from Meerut, then, joining those at Delhi, and being rapidly reinforced from all parts, there soon came to be in the Moghul capital a vast assemblage of well-trained and well-armed troops, fired with fanatic zeal, and doubtless thoroughly conscious of the fact that, having mutinied, there was no turning back. Still it was imagined at first that the British would be able to recapture the place with a small force and with but little effort, but such easy assumption of inevitable instant success for our arms was proved wrong (as it has done again and again within the history of the past few months in South Africa).

In the records of our army there is probably no other siege so remarkable as that of Delhi during the summer of 1857. Here was

a magnificent city some seven miles in cir-
cumference, bounded for about two miles on
one side by the broad waters of the River
Jumna, and surrounded on the others by
massive walls about five-and-twenty feet high,
and with an approach across a ditch some
five-and-twenty feet broad. This city, for
hundreds of years the centre of the great
Moghul Empire, was suddenly wrested from
the dominion of the English, and with its
vast stores of arms and ammunition was
rapidly occupied by regiment after regiment
of mutineers, some of whom got there with
their full equipment, and others, for whom,
though they had been disarmed by the prompt
action of British officers, there was no difficulty in finding material in the plentiful stores
of the Delhi armoury.

At first the Delhi Field Force, entrusted
with the task of retaking the city, consisted of
but about 3,000 men, and at its best it never
counted much above 9,000 efficient com-
batants. This Delhi Field Force, to use the
fine description of one of the historians of the
Indian Mutiny, " having planted its head-

quarters on the site of the old British cantonments on the ' Ridge,' was now spreading
itself out over the ground which it had conquered, in the manner best adapted to both
offensive and defensive operations. Seldom
has a finer position been occupied by a British
army ; seldom has a more magnificent pano-
rama turned for awhile the soldiers' thoughts
from the stern realities of the battle. It was
difficult not to admire the beauty of the scene
even amidst the discomforts of the camp and
the labours of the first encamping. The great
city, with its stately mosques and minarets,
lay grandly at our feet, one side resting on the
Jumna, and others forming a mighty mass of
red walls, standing out threateningly towards
the position which we had occupied. And
scattered all about beneath us were pic-
turesque suburbs and stately houses, walled
gardens and verdant groves, refreshing to the
eye ; whilst the blue waters of the flowing
Jumna glittered in the light of the broad sun.
It was not an hour for philosophical specula-
tion or for the indulgence of any romantic
sentiments concerning the decay of empires

and the revolutions of dynasties; else was there much food for thought in the strange circumstances which had brought a British army to besiege a city which, only a month before, had been regarded as securely our own as London or Liverpool, and to contend against a sovereign who, within the same brief space of time, had been held in contempt as a harmless puppet. There was no room in the minds of our military chiefs for such thoughts as these. They contemplated the position on which they had encamped an army with the keen eyes of practical soldiers, and looked around them from their commanding position upon the ground that was to be the scene of their future operations."[*]

This, then, was the position in which General Barnard's small army was situated when Lieutenant Roberts joined it on June 28th. It was no doubt gratifying to the young soldier to find that he had arrived in time to take part in the capture of the city, for such capture was at first looked upon as likely

[*] "A History of the Sepoy War in India," 1857–1858. By J. W. Kaye.

to be the consequence of a few days' siege—in actual fact, it was to take close upon three months after Roberts took up his duties as D.A.Q.M.G. to the artillery. He heard of the fighting that had taken place since the arrival of the force, and gathered therefrom that he would not have long to wait before seeing some active service. Nor did he; for two days later, on June 30th, the rebels attacked the British at two of the points nearest to the city—for it must be remembered that the besieging force was itself besieged—and then Roberts was under fire for the first time. The enemy were repulsed, as they were again and again, but each such attempt on the part of the enemy cost the English dearly; for although on this occasion but eight men were killed and thirty wounded, still General Barnard's force could ill afford the loss of a single efficient fighter.

This is not the place to follow in detail the thirty-two fights which took place before Delhi was once again captured in September; to recount all the incidents of heroism belonging to that " struggle between a mere handful of men along the open Ridge and a host behind massive and well-fortified walls." It was on July 1st, it may be mentioned, that the first regimental band reached the British force —it was that of the 61st Regiment from Ferozepore—and it marched into camp to the exhilarating strains of " Cheer, Boys, Cheer! "

During many of the fights Roberts attended the leader as staff officer, and was with Major Coke on July 4th, when he commanded the column which prevented the enemy taking Alipur. It was during one of the most memorable days of the siege, on July 14th—just two months before the final assault began— that Roberts got a wound which placed him on the sick list for some time. On this day, as on the last day of June, the mutineers attacked the position at a point known as Hindu Rao's house. Brigadier Showers was given command of the repelling force, and Lieutenant Roberts accompanied him as his staff officer. The enemy had attacked at about eight o'clock in the morning, and all day long the fighting had gone on, both forces being under cover, but in the afternoon the British

took the aggressive side and began to drive
the foe back towards the city. "The enemy
were driven from point to point, in confused
flight, clean out of their sheltering walls; and
the more impetuous of their assailants pushed
on after them along the main road, within the
fire from the walls of Delhi." The retirement proved more hazardous than the advance,
for the enemy at once rallied when they found
the British leaving them. Then it was that
most of the casualties occurred. Roberts was
at the time with the advanced guns, and as
they began to retire he saw some men moving
a sergeant who had been shot in the leg into a
hut by the roadside. Knowing the inhuman
treatment which the mutineers were in the
habit of according to such wounded as fell
into their hands, Lieutenant Roberts, seeing
the unfortunate sergeant about to be put in
the hut, shouted to the men who were
carrying him—

"Don't put him there; he will be left
behind; get a doolie for him, or put him on
the limber."

The considerate advice was unheard in the

din of battle, and the wretched non-commissioned officer and another wounded man put in the hut with him were murdered as soon as the spot was vacated by the English. A few moments later and Roberts was himself wounded. There was great difficulty in limbering up the guns, and the Lieutenant was lending the men a helping hand in keeping the horses quiet during the operation, when he suddenly had the sickening sensation of being struck in the back. He had been hit near the spine, and would have been killed but for the happy accident that a leather pouch, which he usually wore in front, had slipped round to the back and considerably broken the force of the bullet, which consequently did not penetrate far, and he managed fortunately to be able to keep on his horse until safely back within the British lines.

Hodson, of Hodson's Horse, a familiar figure moving through the annals of the Mutiny, in recording the casualties of this day's fight, said: "Chamberlain shot through the arm, and little Roberts."

The wound was not a serious one, but it

was a month before the Deputy-Assistant-Quartermaster-General could again take up his own duties, although the latter half of that month he spent in the prosecution of other essential, if less pleasant, work in the camp.

During the Siege of Delhi there were no fewer than three officers in chief command: General Barnard was carried off by cholera; his successor, General Reed, resigned owing to partial breakdown consequent upon the strain and anxiety of the position; and to the third, General Wilson—thanks to the unwavering support of an indomitable staff —success finally came in mid-September. Shortly after taking up the command General Wilson had written: "It is my firm determination to hold my present position and to resist every attack to the last. The enemy are very numerous, and may possibly break through our entrenchments and overwhelm us. But this force will die at its post." That was the spirit animating all, and that was the spirit which kept officers and men alike enduring all the unutterable horrors of a campaign in a terribly fierce climate against overwhelming odds and against a seemingly impregnable position.

The weeks went on with fighting here and there as the mutineers sallied out from the city and attacked the pickets, or as brave parties of the British—and Roberts was frequently among them—sought information as to points of vantage for themselves and weakness in the enemy's defences almost up to the walls of Delhi. At length, in the middle of September, the bolder spirits in General Wilson's council prevailed, a general assault of the place was decided upon, and all plans carefully laid, each man having his place assigned to him in the scheme. For some time before the attack could be made the engineers and artillery were particularly busy in their preparations, and for a week at a time Lieutenant Roberts was in Battery No. 2, only leaving it for his meals. Here, indeed, on one occasion he experienced a very narrow escape, being actually knocked over by a ball and yet unhurt. New batteries had been placed between the British camp and the city walls, and these were used to effect a breach while a party of devoted men set out to explode one of the great city gates. Graphic accounts of the storming of Delhi have been written by many of the officers who took part in the event, but we cannot linger over the details of the heroic task so heroically accomplished.

The attacking force was formed into four columns, and being on the General's staff Lieutenant Roberts did not join any of these, but was with General Wilson at Ludlow Castle overlooking the whole advance. Fortunately for him, though, he was in at the finish, for he was with the General when he rode into the town after the columns who were stubbornly fighting their way through the city. Rumours came to the commander of disaster to one or other of these columns, and Lieutenant Roberts was sent off to find out the truth, and on his way had the terribly sad experience of seeing for the last time the officer who has been through life his great exemplar as a military leader. His own words best tell the touching incident :—

"Just after starting on my errand, while riding through the Kashmir Gate, I observed by the side of the road a doolie, without bearers, and with evidently a wounded man inside. I dismounted to see if I could be of any use to the occupant, when I found, to my grief and consternation, that it was John Nicholson, with death written on his face. He told me that the bearers had put the doolie down and gone off to plunder; that he was in great pain, and wished to be taken to the hospital. He was lying on his back; no wound was visible, and but for the pallor of his face, always colourless, there was no sign of the agony he must have been enduring. On my expressing a hope that he was not seriously wounded, he said: 'I am dying; there is no chance for me.' The sight of that great man lying helpless and on the point of death was almost more than I could bear. Other men had daily died around me, friends and comrades had been killed beside me, but I never felt as I felt then—to lose Nicholson seemed to me at that moment to lose everything."*

* Lord Roberts' "Forty-one Years in India."

A GROUP OF OFFICERS WITH WHOM LORD ROBERTS HAS BEEN
ASSOCIATED IN WARFARE.

On this day the British had got a firm footing in Delhi, though the capture was by no means complete—indeed, the general in command was doubtful if they could hold what they had got. They did, however, and bit by bit, by indomitable pluck and perseverance, drove the multitudinous enemy from his various strongholds in the city. The fight went on for days, until on September 20th the Palace itself was taken, and at sunrise on the following day " a royal salute proclaimed that we were again masters in Delhi, and that for the second time in the century the great city had been captured by a British force."

The victory had been hardly-wrung and dearly-bought, for, to use the memorable words which close Kaye's " History of the Sepoy War " : " From city to city, from cantonment to cantonment went the chequered tidings : Delhi had fallen, the King was a captive—but John Nicholson was dead."

Before continuing to follow our hero through the story of his other services during the Indian Mutiny we fittingly close this chapter with a brief tribute from the pen of the

officer (Major Brind) who commanded the
Foot Artillery at Delhi : "It was patent to the
Delhi Field Force that this zealous, clever
officer never missed an opportunity of serving
the cause which we were engaged in, and of
laying in a stock of practical knowledge that
proved so valuable to him in after life."

Roberts was also "mentioned in dispatches"
concerning the Siege of Delhi, General
Archdale Wilson speaking of him in the
following terms in the course of his dispatch
written after the capture of Delhi, and dated
September 22nd : "I beg also to bring very
favourably to notice the officers . . . also
that gallant and active officer, Lieutenant
F. S. Roberts, attached to the Artillery
Brigade in the capacity of Deputy-Assistant-
Quartermaster-General." The consequence
of this mention was that in the General Orders
issued by the Governor-General in Council on
November 5, 1857, "Lieutenant F. S. Roberts,
attached to the Artillery Brigade as Deputy-
Assistant-Quartermaster-General," was one of
the officers specially thanked "for zealous
assistance afforded to their commander and to
the State."

CHAPTER IV

After Delhi — Bulandshahr — A narrow escape — On a
wildgoose chase — Ten days at Lucknow — The
heroic relief—Personal incidents.

THE Siege of Delhi was in many ways one
of the most remarkable incidents of the
Indian Mutiny. It had been imagined at first
that a small British force could easily regain
possession of the fine old city. The place
had been taken and retaken several times
before within its history, and no one could
foresee that the mutineers could hold it
for months against European troops, even
though the numbers of the besiegers were far,
far smaller than those of the defenders. It
proved a long and stubborn fight, but patient
bravery, knowing when and how to act,
succeeded in the end, and a great sigh of relief

5

must have gone up all over India at the news
that the English were once again masters of
Delhi. Other places were hard pressed, and
the welcome victory released a number of tried
soldiers, so that they could proceed to the help
of those places where small bodies of Europeans
were encircled by the fanatical enemy. Among
the officers who were thus able to leave Delhi
was Lieutenant Roberts.

On September 21st Delhi fell, and three days
later the general in command detached a force
consisting of 750 British and 1,900 native
soldiers, with 16 guns, to proceed, *viâ* Cawnpore, to join the column formed for the relief
of Lucknow. Colonel Greathed was given the
command of the force, and Roberts went with
him in the same capacity as that in which he
had served during the Siege. They set out
in the early morning, just as the funeral of
the loved leader, John Nicholson, was taking
place, and passed many a gruesome relic of
the terrible struggle which had so recently
terminated.

They had not gone four days on their
journey before they fell in with some of the

enemy near Bulandshahr, and Colonel Bourchier has recorded Roberts' part in the
advance on this place in the following words :
" By the cross-fire which was kept up upon
the enemy's battery, their fire was subdued ;
an advance was then ordered. A few salvoes
of grape cleared the front, and the commanding officer being anxious that the position
should be secured, ordered an immediate
advance of artillery. Lieutenant Roberts of
the artillery, who seemed ubiquitous, brought
the order at a gallop. The guns charged and
took the battery, the enemy scampering before
us as we came up to it. Lieutenant Roberts
was first at the guns. A second burst, after
clearing our front with grape, brought us to the
goal : the enemy flying before us like sheep." *

The enemy was boldly attacked and driven
back into the town and then through it. The
pursuers soon found themselves in some
difficulty in the narrow streets, and Roberts
had a remarkably narrow escape. He was
riding a somewhat restive horse, one that had

* " An Eight Months' Campaign," by Colonel George
Bourchier, C.B.

been the property of his loved friend and commander, Nicholson, and was more or less
inextricably mixed up in a crowd of friends
and foes, when he observed a sepoy deliberately
aiming at him with a musket. Roberts strove
unsuccessfully to get at his enemy, when
his frightened animal reared just at the
critical moment and received in its head the
bullet that had been meant for its master.
The success of the attack on the town was
soon assured, and the enemy fled some distance
away, so that the column began with a happy
omen its long march towards Lucknow.

Before leaving the neighbourhood of
Bulandshahr an amusing adventure befell
Lieutenant Roberts. News was brought to
him of an Englishwoman in distress—kept
in durance vile at a village some twenty
miles away. He at once got permission
from the commander to proceed to her
relief, and set off with a couple of fellow-
officers and two squadrons of cavalry. They
reached the village by early dawn, surrounded
it, and with a small escort, to borrow the
officer's own words, " we three proceeded up

the little street to the house where the guide
told us the lady was confined. Not only was
the house empty, but, with the exception of a
few sick and bedridden old people, there was
not a soul in the village. There had evidently
been a hasty retreat, which puzzled me greatly,
as I had taken every precaution to ensure
secrecy, for I feared that if our intention to
rescue the lady became known she would be
carried off. As day broke we searched the
surrounding crops and found the villagers and
some soldiers hidden amongst them. They
one and all denied that there was the slightest
truth in the story, and as it appeared a waste
of time to further prosecute the fruitless search
we were on the point of starting to rejoin our
camp when there was a cry from our troopers
of ' *Mem sahib hai!* ' (' Here is the lady ! '), and
presently an excessively dusky girl about
sixteen years of age appeared, clad in native
dress. We had some difficulty in getting the
young woman to tell us what had happened ;
but on assuring her that no harm should be
done to those with whom she was living, she
told us that she was the daughter of a clerk

in the Commissioner's office at Vitapur; that all her family had been killed when the rising took place at that station, and that she had been carried off by a sowar to his home. We asked her if she wished to come away with us. After some hesitation she declined, saying the sowar had married her (Mahomedan fashion) and was kind to her, and she had no friends and relations to go to. On asking her why she had sent to let us know she was there, she replied that she thought she would like to join the British force, which she heard was in the neighbourhood, but on further reflection she had come to the conclusion it was best for her to remain where she was. After talking to her for some time, and making quite sure she was not likely to change her mind, we rode away, leaving her to her sowar, with whom she was apparently quite content. I need hardly say we got unmercifully chaffed on our return to camp, when the result of our expedition leaked out." *

Fighting "incidents" occurred in plenty as Colonel Greathed's column continued

* Lord Roberts' "Forty-one Years in India."

its duty of scouring the tract of country known as the Gangetic Doab. Malagarh, deserted by the rebels, was occupied and destroyed; Khurja, too, had been deserted, and the column pressed on to Aligarh, where the enemy made but a brief stand and were routed on October 5th. From Agra "epistles imploring aid, in every language, both dead and living, and in cypher, came pouring into the camp," wrote Colonel Bourchier, whose brief but interesting narrative I have before referred to. Greathed pressed on and reached Agra on October 10th. The men must have been worn and tanned by their long struggle and by exposure, and several accounts of their arrival at Agra describe the appearance which they made. Lord Roberts himself says that they were so bronzed that it was difficult to distinguish the British from the native troops, and he recalls having heard one of the fair residents of Agra say as the column arrived, "Was ever such a dirty-looking lot seen?" A gentleman who was in Agra at the time wrote: "The Queen's 8th passed within three yards of us. 'Those dreadful-looking men must be Afghans,' said a lady to me, as they slowly and wearily marched by. I did not discover they were Englishmen till I saw a short clay pipe in the mouth of nearly the last man. My heart bled to see these jaded, miserable objects, and to think of all they must have suffered since May last, to reduce fine Englishmen to such worn, sun-dried skeletons."

At Agra the English seem to have been suffering from panic combined with carelessness, and though they reported that the enemy were then far away—frightened off by the approach of the column—yet no sooner was camp formed than the fanatic foe attacked in considerable numbers at a time when the English were absolutely unprepared. "Then and there was hurrying to and fro and mounting in hot haste," for all were taken by surprise. Lieutenant Roberts, riding off for his leader, found himself suddenly confronted by one of the mutineers, who, waving a turban in front of the officer's horse, was trying to slash at the rider. The frightened animal would not go near enough for the officer to use his sword and his revolver would not go off, when a lancer coming up in the nick of time, ran the sowar through the body, and Roberts had again come well out with a narrow escape. In the end, despite the suddenness of the surprise, the rebels were beaten off and pursued for some miles.

A Bengal magistrate has described the unpleasant episode in the following manner: "The column after crossing the river had marched on to the great parade ground. There the soldiers pitched their tents and went to breakfast. Relying on the official information they had received that the mutineers were far away, the commanding officers neither threw out pickets nor adopted any other of the usual precautions against surprise. Especially no search was made among the high crops or in the gardens; also the crowds from the city were allowed to flock round the camp—as many as liked to.

"Among these crowds there was a troop of jugglers; they came on throwing balls and doing tricks, and advancing always nearer and nearer towards the tents. Some English lancers and a party of Sikh soldiers were standing watching them. All of a sudden the jugglers jerked away their balls, threw off their juggler's dresses, and displayed themselves as Mohammedan fanatics. They drew their swords, uttered the Mussulman war-cry, and rushed among the tents, slashing right and left. Their shouts appeared to be the signal, for at the same moment two troops of cavalry galloped out from among the tall crops. There was a roar of artillery, and round shot came rolling in from batteries concealed near the Wrestler's Tomb and among the gardens.

" The alarm was so sudden, and the attack so utterly unexpected, that it might have thrown many troops into disorder, but those of the column were fresh from Delhi, and prepared for all the incidents of war. The first momentary confusion over, they behaved with the utmost coolness. The lancers ran to their horses, saddled and mounted ; the infantry seized their muskets, and the artillerymen limbered up the guns. The rebel cavalry had calculated on a surprise, when instead the lancers charged them. They themselves were seized with a panic; they fought for a few minutes, then turned and fled."

Agra was left on October 14th, and the column—the story of which at the time is the story of Roberts—proceeding by way of Mainpuri (where Sir Hope-Grant overtook it and assumed the command) and Bewar reached Cawnpore eleven days later. Here they heard details of the awful massacre which had taken place at the end of June, and must have felt newly anxious to relieve the besieged at Lucknow. Outram and Havelock had relieved Lucknow earlier but with insufficient force, and were themselves besieged. On October 30th Cawnpore was left behind, and Hope-Grant moved on towards Lucknow, halting half-way that the Commander-in-Chief, Sir Colin Campbell (afterwards Lord Clyde), might come up with the column. Roberts and a comrade, with an escort of a couple of sowars, rode off to find a camping ground, and having found it sent the escort back to bring along the camp attendants. The place seemed clear of any suspicious-looking folk, and the young officers were speaking to some passing pilgrims when suddenly a bullet whizzed over their heads, fired from the direction from which they had just come. The surprise was complete, for some few hundred yards away on the road that lay between them and the column was a crowd of armed men! Luckily Roberts and his companion had already reconnoitred the country and knew of the one possible way of escape, and galloped off to their left. The enemy turned in the same direction towards a village which the officers had to pass. The firing got hotter as they neared the village, but by luck they succeeded in skirting it without getting hit. They were just beginning to feel that they had out-distanced their pursuers when they came to the bank of a deep *nulla*. Roberts' companion cleared it, but unfortunately his own horse slipped and rolled with him into the water at the bottom. His plight was a parlous one, for he had cut his hand with his sword in falling, and the blood made the reins so slippery that he found it difficult to get into the saddle again and, having done so, found that the enemy had reached the bank of the *nulla* and were preparing to fire. Forcing his horse through the water and up the opposite bank he galloped into some high vegetation, where his companion had already got under cover. General Hope-Grant had almost given them up, having known that they were ahead and having heard the sounds of firing. "The dear old fellow," says Lord Roberts in recounting this story of his remarkable escape, "evinced his satisfaction at our safe return by shaking each of us heartily by the hand, repeating over and over again in his quick, quaint way, 'Well, my boys, well, my boys, very glad to have you back! never thought to see you again.'"

On November 9th Sir Colin Campbell joined the column, and at length, with a small army reinforced up to nearly five thousand men, set upon that magnificent task —the final relief of Lucknow. Roberts had a part to play in that relief, and he played it well. On the 13th he was delighted when, riding beside Sir Colin on a reconnaissance, he was told that next day he was to be entrusted with the honourable task of conducting the force to the Dilkusha, where the commander had determined to encamp his forces *en route* for the Residency, in which the handful of Europeans were sorely beset by the enemy, and where they had been confined during so many weeks of terrible agony and anxiety. The following day came and Lieutenant Roberts satisfactorily acquitted himself of the task entrusted him, so that by noon the Dilkusha Park and the Martiniere, a building nearer the canal, which had to be crossed, were occupied, although this was by no means accomplished without a good deal of fighting. It is impossible, as I have said before, to follow the story of the Mutiny, except at those points at which it concerns the life-story of Lord Roberts, but it also is impossible in a small volume like this to follow the details of the chief episodes in which he was directly concerned. The story of the Relief of Lucknow would fill a large volume—has indeed been told and retold in many volumes—and we must here pass hurriedly over it, although one other incident concerning Roberts' personal share in it must not be omitted.

After a hard day's work on November 15th Lieutenant Roberts was summoned to the presence of the Commander-in-Chief, and was told by Sir Colin that he was not satisfied that a sufficient reserve of ammunition for the small arms had been brought forward. The only chance of getting more was to send back to the Alambagh for it. Did Roberts think he could find his way there in the dark?

"I am sure I can," was the ready reply of the young officer, who had (as he thought) taken the precaution to secure the man who had acted as his guide on the day before, in case his services should be needed.

He was at once entrusted with the task, Sir Colin Campbell having impressed upon him the necessity for the greatest caution, and told him to take what escort he thought necessary. All arrangements were completed, when to Roberts' consternation his native guide had disappeared! However distrustful

he might be of himself without the aid of
that guide, he had to see the matter through,
and so, accompanied by a couple of other
young officers (and the ordnance officer who
was at fault) he set out at nine o'clock at
night with an escort consisting of two squadrons of native cavalry and one hundred and
fifty camels, upon which to bring back the
ammunition. It must have been an exciting
experience, for the little force found themselves at times dangerously near the enemy's
pickets—so near that they could hear them
talking. Then, good fortune having so far
attended them that when the night was nearly
half through they were really nearing the Alambagh, Roberts thought that they might be
fired on by their friends. He therefore went
on alone, leaving the rest at some distance,
hailed a sentry, and after some parleying saw
the officer on duty, and arranged with him
that the ammunition boxes should be ready
for lading when he returned. Then he rode
back and brought his little procession to the
Alambagh. The lading-up was rapidly proceeded with, and the silent, backward march

was soon begun, for the Commander-in-Chief had impressed upon Roberts the absolute necessity of his being before Lucknow again by daybreak. The day had dawned as the cavalcade approached the camp, and it was broad daylight by the time that the young officer had made over the precious load to the proper officers and went to the headquarters to Sir Colin Campbell, whom he found "only partially dressed, standing on the steps in evident anxiety."

Cordially the old soldier complimented the young one on the success of his little expedition, and the younger might be excused for feeling some pride in having won the commendation of the veteran. That same day a forward movement was made and Roberts was soon in the thick of the struggle, which after several days' arduous fighting against terrific odds resulted in the final relief of Lucknow and the removal of the women and children and the heroic garrison to a place of safety.

Of the incidents directly concerned with the life-story of Frederick Sleigh Roberts

the following must be mentioned, illustrating
as it does in the person of the present Field-
Marshal the dogged perseverance by which
British soldiers have so often succeeded
against heavy numerical odds. When the
last position which divided the beleaguered
from the relieving force was secured, Sir
Colin Campbell ordered Roberts to place a
regimental colour on one of the turrets of
the building (the mess house). The young
officer at once obeyed, secured one of the
colours of the 2nd Punjab Infantry, and
galloping off with it, got it up to the turret
and made it secure. This signal to those
beleagured in the Residency was at once seen
by the enemy, who immediately directed their
fire towards it, and in a few minutes it was
hit and fell over into the ditch below. Roberts
instantly ran down and got it, and then put it
up again, but it was again knocked over. Yet
again he descended, and for the third time
fastened it on the turret, where it remained,
though freely fired at by the enemy. Another
fact that calls for special mention here is
that Roberts was one of the two officers of

the relieving force who met the heroes of the
first relief, Sir James Outram and Sir Henry
Havelock, and escorted them to Sir Colin
Campbell, was present at the memorable
meeting of the three heroes, and returned
with Outram and Havelock to the Residency,
so that he was among the earliest of the
relief column to get inside that historic
place.

After the "Relief" had been accomplished
came the arduous task of getting the rescued
people away, for Sir Colin Campbell recognised
the impossibility of taking Lucknow from the
rebels, and therefore, as quietly as possible,
withdrew, having accomplished his great
task. The besieging of the city was left to
be carried out later when he had a bigger force
at his command.

The retreat was in a sense more dangerous
than the advance, and it had to be effected
at night so as to minimise the possibility of the
mutineers becoming aware of it. Here again
Roberts' courage was again usefully put to
the test. That the retirement of the different
brigades should be simultaneous was, of course,

a vital necessity, and an officer of one of these rear brigades was kept with the headquarters staff that he might ride back to his General and acquaint him with the moment for starting. At the right moment General Mansfield, Chief of the Staff, told this officer what to do, but he replied that he did not think he could find his way! On this Mansfield was, and with reason, very angry, and turning to Roberts, said—

"You have been to Hale's position; do you think you could find your way there now?"

Roberts, who must have had a genius for finding his way about in the dark, answered with soldierly readiness, "I think I can." He was sent off on the hazardous duty accompanied by the more timid officer; but though he had only been over the ground twice before, though the intervening villages had been destroyed and there was no road, the officers managed to get through all right. Then having delivered his message Lieutenant Roberts had to find his way back alone to where he had left the General and his Staff.

When he reached the spot they had gone! How long and how far he could only surmise. His position was not a pleasant one, but, fortunately for him, the enemy had not discovered that the British army had "silently stolen away," and he therefore galloped on what he knew to be the line of retirement, where before long he overtook the straggling column.

From when they left the Alambagh on November 14th until they got back to it on November 24th officers and men alike had been working almost without cessation. "A wash and a change of clothes" became possible for the first time for ten days, and Lord Roberts, recalling that great event in which he had borne a genuinely useful part, has said that, despite the roughness of the experience, the incessant exposure, and the brief snatches of sleep which were obtainable, he was in the best of health, and that though he "almost lived on horseback" he never felt inconvenience or fatigue.

CHAPTER V

ON the very day that the first part of Sir
Colin Campbell's force reached the
Alambagh, there passed away one of the brave
heroes of the first Relief, who had lived
just long enough to be taken from the place
which he had so nobly succoured a few weeks
earlier. It was on November 26th that a
mournful group committed to the earth all
that remained of Sir Henry Havelock.

General Outram, with his brigade, was left
to hold the Alambagh and thus prevent the
Lucknow rebels from descending on Cawnpore,
while another force was left at some distance
to support him in case of need, and then, "On
the morning of the 27th, leaving these
detachments in his rear, Sir Colin Campbell,

hampered as no army ever was before, with a train extending along at least ten miles of road, three deep, started for Cawnpore, to see what mischief was brewing in that direction." Firing had been heard from the neighbourhood of Cawnpore, but as to what might be happening there no one could tell, until just before noon on the 28th, as they were pressing forward, a native delivered a note to the advance guard. The note was directed to Sir Colin, "or any officer commanding troops on the Lucknow road." It declared that the troops at Cawnpore were in serious straits and in urgent need of help.

On the receipt of this news, says an eye-witness, "the impatience and anxiety of all became extreme. Louder and louder grew the roar—faster and faster became the march—long and weary was the way—tired and footsore grew the infantry—death fell on the exhausted wounded with terrible rapidity—the travel-worn bearers could hardly stagger along under their loads—the sick men groaned and died—but still on, on, on, was the cry." *

* *Blackwood's Magazine*, October, 1858.

Early in the afternoon of that day Sir Colin
Campbell's impatience was such, that having
fired three salvoes of artillery to give notice of
his proximity, he hurried forward with his
staff, fearful that the bridge of boats across the
Ganges might have been destroyed—that some
irretrievable disaster might have occurred
before his succours could arrive.   He sent
Lieutenant Roberts on ahead, and great was
the gratification of that officer when he saw
the bridge of boats still intact.   He found that
General Windham had been compelled to
leave the city and stores to the enemy, and
retire with his inadequate force to the
entrenchments near the river, although he was
able to hold the foe sufficiently in check to
prevent the destruction of the bridge of boats.
The General himself was alert and hopeful, but
his troops were terribly dispirited, and the
news of the near arrival of Sir Colin Campbell
and his force was warmly welcomed.   Having
ascertained all that he could, Roberts was
about to return to Sir Colin, but that officer's
impatience had been too great to allow of his
waiting for his messenger's return, and he had

hurried on after him. Roberts then returned
to the camp about four miles on the Lucknow
side of the river, where his own General (Hope.
Grant) was for the time being situated. The
next morning an advance was made, and Sir
Colin could congratulate himself, as Colonel
Bourchier put it, on having "performed one
of the most difficult of military operations,
crossing a wide river in the face of an enemy
thoroughly equipped with artillery," the division to which Roberts was attached being told
off to take up such a position as would keep
open the road from Cawnpore to Allahabad—
an important measure, seeing that it was there
that the women and children and wounded
rescued from Lucknow had to be sent. This
necessitated several days of reconnoitring with
the cavalry, but the real decisive conflict was
not long delayed.

On December 3rd the wounded and women
were sent off to Allahabad, and then the field
hospital was established and other preparations
made for the attack. For six days, as one of
the officers put it, the British troops were
chafing and fretting with an impatient desire

to be let loose against the foe, whose pickets were in some cases but about a hundred and twenty yards away, and whose shot "kept continually bowling into the camp." At length the English commander had completed his plans and the disposition of his troops, and early on the morning of December 6th he explained to his officers the course of the day's operations. His plans, well laid, were carried out almost without a hitch, and as the historian of the war has said, " the battle established the right of Sir Colin Campbell to be regarded as a great commander." The enemy were, after a fierce attack at three points, put to flight and thoroughly routed. With less than 6,000 men, an enemy numbering 25,000 were effectually defeated. When the attack had begun, Sir Colin Campbell and Sir Hope Grant, with their respective staffs—in which of course Roberts had his place—went with the force that fell on the enemy's camp. The camp was soon cleared and orders given for the pursuit: "Hurrah! hurrah! we are on their track; gun after gun is passed and spiked, cartloads of ammunition lay strewed along the road; Pandies are bolting in all directions. For two miles without a check the pursuit was carried on by the battery alone, accompanied by Sir Hope Grant and his staff. Four times in that distance did we come into action, to clear our front and flanks; until General Grant, thinking wisely that we were too far from our supports, determined to wait until the cavalry arrived. A halt was called, not until it was required, for the horses, though in the condition of racers, had felt the pace. A small cloud coming nearer and nearer is seen on the left. The head of the cavalry column debouches from a grove. The order for a further pursuit is given. The cavalry spread like lightning over the plain, in skirmishing order. Sir Colin takes the lead. The pursuit is continued to the fourteenth milestone; assuming all the character of a fox-hunt. Strange to say, not many miles beyond the enemy's camp a fox broke right in front of the enemy's column, and a view halloa told Reynard that the heavy crops would be his safest refuge. At the fourteenth milestone, on the banks of the

Pandoo River, the pursuit ceased, not a trace, either of an enemy or a cart of any kind, being in sight."

The rout was complete, and when Sir Hope-Grant sent Lieutenant Roberts back to Cawnpore to select a bivouacking ground the highly exciting chase had come to a natural end, for those of the enemy who were not killed had thrown away arms and uniform in the hope that they might pass for innocent peasants.

Next morning it was found that part of the Cawnpore force, that within the city, had succeeded in getting away, and the duty of following up this portion of the enemy's army was entrusted, much to his own and his staff's delight, to Sir Hope-Grant. One day's rest was given and then shortly after noon on December 8th the force started. To Roberts, in carrying out his duties as quartermaster, it fell to find out whither the foe had gone, and he had the good fortune to get hold of an admirable native guide who had proved his loyalty again and again and who subsequently afforded much help. The enemy were caught up with just as they were about to cross the river, were put to flight and had their fifteen guns captured without any loss on the British side. Sir Hope-Grant was next told off to destroy the rebels' stronghold at Bithur, and this, too, was satisfactorily performed. That being, done Roberts had a few days' rest at Cawnpore.

On the 23rd a forward movement was begun again, this time towards Fategarh, with the object of opening up communications with Bengal and the Punjab and also in furtherance of the original design of the column told off from Delhi of restoring order in that tract of country known as the Doab. On the first day of the New Year (1858) the troops halted, and early on the following morning the Commander-in-Chief went forward, but he soon ascertained that the enemy were prepared to make a stand a little way ahead and at once sent back to Hope-Grant to bring on the main body of the troops. This must have been a welcome order to the dashing general, and no less welcome to his staff-officer, who was all unconsciously within

a few hours of earning the much coveted
honour of the Victoria Cross. Forward the
troops went with a will and soon caught up
with the advanced guard, and charging upon
the enemy completely broke them. " Then
despair seized upon the rebel mass; breaking
their ranks, throwing aside their arms, they
fled in wild confusion; but the horsemen
were upon them and amongst them. The
slaughter was terrible; for several miles they
rode along spearing and cutting down at
every step; and the progress of their swift
advance might be marked by the smoke of
exploded tumbrils curling up amidst the dark-
green trees."

Forward among the horsemen dealing
destruction on the flying rebels during a five
miles' pursuit, was Lieutenant Roberts, to
whom at the very end of the chase, just as it
was about to be given up and as dusk was
beginning to come on, came the opportunity
so eagerly longed for by brave soldiers.
Riding alongside an officer friend he saw
that friend fall, and was about to turn to his
assistance when he saw a native soldier in

HOW LIEUTENANT ROBERTS WON THE VICTORIA CROSS.

deadly peril from a rebel who was about to bayonet him, quickly Roberts galloped to the assistance of the hard pressed sowar and then, having cut down his opponent, he saw a couple of the rebels at some distance making off with a standard. Instantly determining that the standard must be captured, he put spurs to his horse and galloped after them, caught them up, and seized hold of the staff, and as he wrenched it from the sepoy's grasp cut him down. He had an almost miraculous escape, for the other sepoy fired a musket close against him, but by a lucky chance it missed fire and the plucky Lieutenant rode back in triumph with the standard, to gain which he had risked everything. This it was which won for him the right to be numbered among the honoured wearers of the " V.C."

The statement of these acts is officially set forth in the following words : "Lieutenant Roberts' gallantry has on every occasion been most marked. On following up the retreating enemy on the 2nd of January, 1858, at Khodagnage, he saw in the distance two sepoys going away with a standard.

Lieutenant Roberts put spurs to his horse, and overtook them just as they were about to enter a village. They immediately turned round and presented their muskets at him, and one of the men pulled the trigger, but fortunately the cap snapped, and the standard-bearer was cut down by the gallant young officer, and the standard taken possession of by him. He also, on the same day, cut down another sepoy who was standing at bay, with musket and bayonet, keeping off a sowar. Lieutenant Roberts rode to the assistance of the horseman, and rushing at the sepoy, with one blow of his sword cut him across the face, killing him on the spot."

Nearly a month was spent at Fategarh while plans for the next important move were matured. This move, it was finally resolved, should be the capture of Lucknow, which had of course continued in the hands of the rebels, who, numbering some thirty thousand at the time of the Relief in November, had been reinforced up to not much short of a hundred thousand by the time of the Siege in March. This ever-growing force had been held in check by Sir James Outram with some four thousand troops at the Alambagh.

In the force designed for the siege of Lucknow Sir Hope-Grant was given the command of the cavalry division, and again he selected Lieutenant Roberts to be his Deputy-Assistant - Quartermaster - General. During February they were kept busy in clearing the country to the north of the Cawnpore-Lucknow road, and a couple of incidents of this expedition which are told by Lord Roberts in his fascinating volume must here have passing mention. They had attacked and taken a small fortified town, and Roberts was superintending the destruction of the fortifications when, to use his own words, "the horrors of war were once more brought very forcibly before me by the appearance of an infirm old man, who besought me to spare his house, saying, 'Yesterday I was the happy father of five sons: three of them lie there' (pointing to a heap of dead bodies); 'where the other two are God only knows. I am old and a cripple, and if my house is burned there is nothing left for me but to die.' Of course I took care that

7

his house and property were untouched." The
other incident was Roberts and a fellow-officer,
who had followed an antelope for some miles,
fleeing campwards from a body of the enemy's
cavalry which they thought to be in close
pursuit of them, but which vanished as rapidly
and mysteriously as they had appeared, and
which were indeed nothing but a *mirage*, an
atmospheric reflection of men probably very
many miles away !

During the first week of March Roberts,
with his General, reached the Alambagh, where
Hope-Grant was given charge of the pickets,
and where his young staff-officer, who always
accompanied him on his rounds, gained much
valuable practical knowledge of outpost duties.
On the 2nd of March they had reached the
scene of the operations, and thenceforward
until the final capture of the city on the 21st,
Lieutenant Roberts was actively engaged in
the assault upon it. The siege and capture
of Lucknow struck such a blow as meant the
final suppression of the Indian Mutiny. Fighting was still necessary, and was still continued,
but some of those who had borne noble parts

in a struggle that had already lasted for close upon a year could claim a well-earned rest.

Lieutenant Roberts had been suffering from the protracted and severe strain of the campaign, and had been medically advised to rest, but pluckily refused to do so until Lucknow was finally in the hands of the British. By that time it was imperative that he should seek a change of climate, and the doctor insisted upon his obtaining a lengthened leave and returning to England. On the 1st of April—six years to a day after his arrival in India—he handed over his duties as D.A.Q.G. to his successor, Major Wolseley (now Field-Marshal Viscount Wolseley, Commander-in-Chief), and shortly afterwards left Lucknow for home. Before his departure, the young officer had the gratification of being thanked by the Commander-in-Chief for his services, Sir Colin promising to take the earliest opportunity of giving him the rank of a Brevet-Major, and also of selecting him for the first permanent vacancy which should occur in the Quartermaster-General's Department.

On May 4th Lieutenant Roberts left

Calcutta on board the steamer *Nubia*, having
during his first half-dozen years in India seen
more of fighting than many soldiers see in a
lifetime, and having won golden opinions from
commanding officers for his display of those
qualities which make the best soldier and the
best leader of soldiers. Six years before he
had left England a cadet, eager and ambitious;
he was returning with rapid promotion in view,
and with an established reputation for courage
and capacity.

For his share in the suppression of the
Indian Mutiny Lord Roberts wears, besides
the most valued of all a soldier's decorations,
the Victoria Cross, a medal with three clasps,
indicating that he played his part in the three
chief acts of that great tragedy—the Siege of
Delhi, the Relief of Lucknow, and the Siege
of Lucknow.

CHAPTER VI

Home on leave—Marriage—Back to the East—The
Umbeyla Expedition—Sick leave again—Fresh
prospect of active service.

HAVING travelled across the Continent
by easy stages, the young Mutiny hero
was, we may be sure, cordially welcomed home
when he reached Waterford at about the end
of June, 1858. There his father, the veteran
soldier with fifty years' knowledge of Indian
service, must have followed the course of the
Mutiny with particular interest and anxiety,
and must have felt peculiar gratification at
the knowledge that he had given to the army
so promising a son. That son had earned a
rest, and he passed some months in Ireland in
the enjoyment of country life, hunting frequently, as so accomplished a horseman might

be expected to do. So passed the autumn of 1858, and the winter that saw that year merge into the next. During his stay at Waterford on this term of leave, too, Lieutenant Roberts met and fell in love with, in the friend of a married sister of his, the lady who shortly afterwards became his bride, and has shared his fortunes and his troubles for over forty years. This lady was Miss Nora Henrietta, daughter of Captain Bews, of the 73rd Foot.

The young couple were married in the parish church of Waterford on May 17, 1859, and set off on a wedding tour in Scotland—a tour which was, however, interrupted by a summons to the young soldier to attend at Buckingham Palace on June 8th, that Her Majesty the Queen might decorate him with the Victoria Cross.

In view of his marriage the officer had applied for three months' extension of his leave, and was told that he could have it, but that by doing so he would lose a promised post in the Quartermaster-General's Department, and would consequently have to wait for another vacancy. Such a chance was not to be missed, and therefore the young couple decided to start for the East forthwith, and they sailed for Calcutta at the end of June, just a year after Roberts' arrival home. The journey out was a terribly trying one, the heat in the Red Sea being phenomenal even for that notoriously hot place ; then, too, their vessel had to battle with a monsoon before they could get a pilot on board to take it up the Hoogli to Calcutta, which was finally reached at the end of July.

At first Roberts was ordered to join the Staff of Sir Robert Napier, then in command of the Gwalior district, but when on his way to take up his duties he was ordered back to Calcutta, to which place he returned in the best of spirits, thinking that he was about to be appointed to the projected Chinese Expedition. Far other was the work for which he was wanted. It was to take part in Lord Canning's progress through the country which was to mark the taking over by Her Majesty the Queen of the dominions which had been ruled by the East India Company. It was by no means an easy task which the young officer had to undertake—the organising and laying out of a movable camp, or pair of camps, for close upon twenty thousand people! The starting camp had to be (and was) ready for occupation on October 15th, but no sooner was one camp occupied than the next had to be prepared so that the Viceroy, his officers, attendants, escort, &c., on arriving at the end of a day's journey would find an exact duplicate of the camp they had left. This necessitated a constant stream of people and baggage carts and animals over four and twenty miles of road at a time. Constant and onerous as was the work, the indefatigable young Q.M.G. acquitted himself well of the multifarious duties connected with his gigantic task. The Viceroy's tour lasted for six months, and the great camp was broken up on April 9, 1860. "Thus ended a six months' march over a thousand miles—a march never likely to be undertaken again by any other Viceroy of India, now that railway trains run from Calcutta to Peshawar, and saloon carriages have taken the place of big tents."

Roberts would have been selected for service

with the China Expedition—an expedition in
which Lord Wolseley served, and of which he
wrote the history, and in which Sir Redvers
Buller, as an ensign, saw service for the first
time—only Lord Clyde thought that it would
be unkind to select an officer who had been so
recently married, and did not give his reasons
until it was too late, much to Roberts' chagrin
and disappointment.

A month before the Viceroy's camp had
been broken up a daughter was born to
Lieutenant Roberts at Mian Mir, and he
journeyed there and took his wife and child
up to Simla, where they remained for the rest
of the year, but for an autumn excursion
further up into the hills. At the beginning
of November Roberts had to organise another
Viceregal camp, but on a much smaller scale
than the earlier one. Certain changes in
the organisation of the Indian Army brought
rapid promotion for some of the officers, and
among these was Lieutenant Roberts, who
became Captain Roberts on November 12th
and Brevet-Major a day later.

At the end of February of the following

year Major Roberts returned to his duties in
the Quartermaster-General's office at Simla,
and a day or two after his arrival he and his
wife suffered their first poignant sorrow in the
death of their first-born child within a few
days of completing her first year.

The new Commander-in-Chief in India was
Sir Hugh Rose, and at his desire the Headquarters' Staff was maintained at Simla, a
much more salubrious spot than in the plains,
and there the year was passed in a quiet
round of duties and home life until October,
when Major Roberts was once more called
upon to establish a camp for the Viceroy.
This time it was to be at Allahabad where the
first investiture of the new Order of the Star
of India was held. After that camp was
broken up Major Roberts accompanied the
Commander-in-Chief on a round of inspection
of the military stations in the Punjab and the
North of India. The next year or two were
marked by the serious illness of both the busy
officer and his wife, and in January, 1863,
Major Roberts had a slight attack of sun-
stroke, the results of which he continued to

feel for a long time. During 1863 he was appointed Assistant Quartermaster-General. In autumn of the same year the Commander-in-Chief telegraphed to his Headquarters' Staff to join him at Mian Mir, where he was with the new Viceroy, Lord Elgin. When Roberts and his colleagues arrived they found that the Viceroy was in a dying state, and that a threatening situation had suddenly arisen on the frontier beyond Peshawar, with possible Afghan developments.

During the autumn of 1863 a small expedition of about five thousand men had been sent into the mountains beyond the north-west frontier of India and on the confines of Afghanistan with the object of punishing certain tribes who had been committing depredations in the border districts. The arrival of the expedition roused other tribes in the neighbourhood, and "the force had to fight hard to maintain its ground and accomplish its purpose." The Commander-in-Chief in November despatched Major Roberts and Colonel Adye (now General Sir John Adye, C.B.), to ascertain all the facts of the case as

to what had happened and was happening to
Sir Neville Chamberlain's expedition. When
the officers arrived on the spot and had
examined the situation they recommended
that reinforcements should be sent up and a
decisive action brought about as the best safeguard for future peace. Their advice tallied
with the views of the Commander-in-Chief,
and a new commander was sent up to take the
place of Chamberlain, who had been severely
wounded. The advance was made under
General Garvock, and on December 15th and
16th the tribes were effectually beaten.
Major Roberts was with the Mountain Battery,
leading the way, and that he must have had
an exciting time of it we may gather from the
brief history of the "little war" which was
written by his companion, Colonel Adye. The
two days' fighting proved sufficient for the
tribes who took part in it, and had an excellent
effect on others who were watching the issue
from the surrounding mountains, and who
would have joined in at once on the first sign
of a reverse to the British troops. As Colonel
Adye puts it: "The effect of these actions

was immediate and decisive. The men of Bajour and Dher, who had come so far and were so eager for war, now fled to their native fastnesses. The Akhoond and his followers were no more to be seen, and the chiefs of Bonair, relieved from the presence of over-bearing allies, gladly came into camp and agreed to terms of peace."*

The terms of peace were that the Bonair tribesmen (or Bunerwals, for in the spelling of these names there is a plentiful lack of unan-imity among writers) should go and destroy the village of Malka, the village of the fanatics who had brought about the trouble. This village was about twenty-five miles away from the scene of the fighting, and a small band of plucky officers agreed to go with them to see that it was done. These seven officers included both Roberts and Adye, and with a small escort they proceeded to Malka and saw the village destroyed. It was indeed a hazar-dous adventure and one that might have had far-reaching consequences, for at any moment

* "Sitana. A Mountain Campaign on the Borders of Afghanistan in 1863." By Colonel John Adye.

the angry tribes might have attacked and massacred the party of men who had so courageously put themselves at their mercy. "This final act of the war," says Colonel Adye, in the small volume from which I have before quoted, "was witnessed by a crowd of mountaineers belonging to the minor tribes of the Mahabun, who gradually collected near the spot and angrily watched the conflagration. There was sorrow as well as anger in their hearts. In their villages were many fresh graves of relatives who had fallen during the campaign; and what also deeply moved them was the hated presence of Englishmen in a part of the country hitherto sacred from intrusion. As there seemed a possibility of their proceeding to acts of violence, they were addressed both by the Commissioner (Colonel Reynell Taylor, C.B.) and by an influential chief of the Bonair, and at length they went silently and sullenly to their homes, and the English officers, with their escort, marched back to the Chumla valley."

It was certainly a very dangerous undertaking, and the little party had a much narrower

escape than would be imagined from reading
Colonel Adye's simple narrative; indeed, at
one time, as the Colonel's companion has
recorded, the attitude of the tribes was so
ominous that "at this moment one of the
Bunerwals came to our rescue. The most
influential of the tribe, a grey-bearded warrior,
who had lost an eye and an arm in some tribal
contest, forced his way through the rapidly-
increasing crowd to Taylor's side, and, raising
his one arm to enjoin silence, delivered himself as follows: 'You are hesitating whether
you will allow these English to return un-
molested. You can, of course, murder them
and their escort, but if you do, you must kill
us Bunerwals first, for we have sworn to
protect them, and we will do so with our
lives.' "

The expedition then returned to the
Umbeyla pass and thence, early in 1864, to
Peshawar, where the headquarters remained
until the end of February. In this same year,
too, Sir Hugh Rose sent in Roberts' name for
a "brevet" as reward for his services with the
Umbeyla Expedition, but the Viceroy stopped

it on the ground "that Major Roberts was
'too junior to be made a lieutenant-
colonel.'"

During the whole of 1864, Major Roberts
suffered from ill-health, which was accentuated
by office work at Simla and by overwork
consequent upon his having undertaken, in
addition to his ordinary duties, the revision
of the "Bengal Route Book." He was
ordered home on sick leave, and he and his wife
left Simla for Calcutta at the end of October.
At Calcutta, Major Roberts was busily engaged
for some time in making arrangements for
transporting a number of troops home, and it
was in charge of the troops on board a transport that he sailed from Calcutta in the following February.

An incident that preceded his departure
is so eminently characteristic of the man,
and also serves to account for the strong
feeling of devotion for him which troops
that he has commanded feel, that I cannot
refrain from giving it in the simple fashion
in which he himself has told it: "At the
inspection parade, before we embarked, a

certain number of men were brought up for punishment for various offences committed on the way down country. None of the misdemeanours appeared to me very serious, so I determined to let the culprits off. I told the men that we had now met for the first time, and I was unwilling to commence our acquaintance by awarding punishments; we had to spend three or four months together, and I hoped they would show, by their good behaviour while under my command, that I had not made a mistake in condoning their transgressions. The officers seemed somewhat surprised at my action in this matter, but I think it was proved by the men's subsequent conduct that I had not judged them incorrectly, for they all behaved in quite an exemplary manner throughout the voyage."

A voyage from India round the Cape was not a rapid journey in those days, and it was May 29th when the transport reached the Lizard, and May 30th when Major Roberts and his wife landed at Portsmouth "between two showers of snow," and learned from a first glimpse at an English newspaper the gratify-

· ing intelligence that his father had just been gazetted a K.C.B.

This time Major Roberts had not quite so long a stay in England as before, and in March, 1866, he sailed for India once again, leaving his wife to follow later in the year. Sir Hugh Rose had been succeeded as Commander-in-Chief by Sir William Mansfield (who had been Chief of the Staff to Sir Colin Campbell during the Mutiny), and Roberts was ordered to join the staff at Allahabad. In October Mrs. Roberts arrived from England, and nearly a year was passed at Allahabad during a serious cholera visitation. In August, 1867, they went to Simla, Roberts hoping to get a post in connection with the projected Abyssinian Expedition. In September he had the welcome news that he had been appointed Assistant-Quartermaster-General to Colonel Donald Stewart (now Field - Marshal Sir Donald Stewart), who was to have the command of the Bengal Brigade with that expedition which was to be under the leadership of Sir Robert Napier.

CHAPTER VII

The Abyssinian Campaign — Promotion and a new appointment — The Lushai Expedition—C.B.— Public ceremonials — Command of the Frontier Force.

GRATIFYING as it was to Major Roberts to find himself selected for service in connection with the Abyssinian Expedition, he was not to take part in the great march to Magdala, which has made famous the name of Lord Napier (then Sir Robert). During the closing weeks of 1867, the officer was busily engaged in arranging for the transport of destined forces to engage in the expedition, which was being undertaken with the object of releasing a number of European and other prisoners kept at his far-off capital by King Theodore of Abyssinia.

Major Roberts was carrying out his duties at Calcutta, and found this work seriously interfered with by a great monsoon, which visited the place and destroyed a lot of the shipping. However, the difficulties were finally surmounted, and at last he set sail for the Red Sea with General Donald Stewart and the rest of that officer's staff. Zula, in Annesley Bay, which was their port of disembarkation, was reached on Febuary 3, 1868. Sir Robert Napier, who was in command of the expedition, had arrived earlier and had begun his forward movement leaving somewhat disappointing orders for the latest arrivals. These orders were that General Stewart was to remain in command of all troops in Zula, or in the mountain passes a few miles on the long journey to the Abyssinian capital, and that Major Roberts was to remain with him as his Assistant Quartermaster-General.

A soldier's first duty is to obey, and if Major Roberts, not unnaturally, regretted missing a chance of being at the front, he was too good a soldier to repine over it, and he cheerfully

set about his manifold duties at Sir Robert
Napier's base. And arduous those duties
must have been, seeing the strength of the
force which it had been necessary to equip
for the purpose of maintaining a line of
communications for an army which had to
journey about three hundred and eighty miles.
The climate was a notoriously bad one, and
the heat at Zula was terrible, but although
there were landing points available nearer to
Magdala this particular one was chosen "for
its fine, commodious harbour, its proximity
to the mountains, and for its water supplies."
These water supplies—except in the mountains fourteen or fifteen miles away—were,
however, nothing to boast of, and that Major
Roberts must have had a fairly trying time
of it during his stay may be gathered from
the histories which have been written of the
Abyssinian campaign.

In the middle of April Magdala was seized
and destroyed, the prisoners were released,
and King Theodore committed suicide. The
expedition having thus come to an end the
troops returned as rapidly as possible to Zula

and were sent thence. At the beginning of June Napier reached the port, and that he was well satisfied with the manner in which Major Roberts had acquitted himself of his valuable if not "showy" duties is made plain by the fact that he selected him to be the bearer of his final despatches home. On June 10th they sailed, Roberts suffering in health from the combined hard work and severe climate. At Alexandria he was handed the despatches and hurried forward with them, reaching London on the evening of Sunday, June 28th. A despatch bearer has of course to deliver his missives at any hour, and Major Roberts found the Duke of Cambridge (the Commander-in-Chief) at dinner, the Prince and Princess of Wales being his guests, and having presented his papers from Sir Robert Napier he was called upon to tell their Royal Highnesses all that he could about the " little war" which had been brought to so brilliant a conclusion.

When he left Calcutta for Zula, Major Roberts had taken his wife with him as far as Aden, and thence she had returned to England;

and having completed his official duties he then joined his family at Clifton, a daughter having been born to him shortly after his arrival from Abyssinia. On the publication in mid-August of the list of honours and promotions gained for service with the Abyssinian Expedition, Major Roberts found himself promoted to a Brevet Lieutenant-Colonel.

After a few months of rest Colonel Roberts was once more preparing to return to India, and on January 4, 1869, he left Portsmouth with his wife and child. The voyage proved a very sad one, for the little girl died before they reached their destination.

Colonel Roberts arrived at Simla, and his five years as Assistant-Quartermaster-General coming to an end, he applied for the command of a battery of Horse Artillery, being desirous of going back to his old regiment. His application was approved, and he was duly appointed to a battery at Meerut, but before long he was offered another Staff appointment—the post, which had then been newly created, of First Assistant-Quartermaster-General—which post he promptly accepted. A

Staff appointment had the great advantage of
allowing of residence at Simla, where there
was at once a more healthful climate and a
better chance of congenial society than at a
smaller station.

The next two years passed in the quiet
exercise of official duties at headquarters, and
during this time the officer "amused" himself
by going through a course of electric tele-
graphy, having determined, when a hitch
had occurred in the telegraphic arrangements
during the Umbeyla Expedition, that he
would learn how to use the telegraph himself,
so that he should be able to send or receive
messages if a similar difficulty arose in the
future. This incident serves to suggest something of the character of the man, who cares
for no trouble so that he can increase his
self-reliance.

In the summer of 1871 came news of the pre-
paration for a new expedition into the country
of the Lushais—tribes who had caused some
trouble by their raids upon the tea plantations,
and who, among other offences, had taken
prisoner a little English girl. The tract of

country occupied by the Lushais is situated
between Bengal and Burma, and the depredations of the tribes had become so serious
that the Lieutenant-Governor of Bengal had
declared that an expedition " was absolutely
necessary for the future security of the British
subjects residing on the Cachar and Chitta-
gong frontiers."

A punitive expedition was decided upon,
and the force was to be divided into two
columns, with Colonel Roberts as chief staff
officer.   Before the force could start, however,
there was a great deal of work to be done at
Calcutta, Roberts' orders being "to fit out
and despatch the two columns and then join
General Bourchier at Cachar."   After several
weeks of hard work he got away about the
middle of November, and then began one of
those " little wars" which, however insignifi-
cant they may appear in the few lines accorded
to them in the history-books, are significant of
much as educational factors to the tribes on
the fringe of our empire, and also to the soldiers
taking part in them.

The Lushai Expedition had to proceed

through a trackless country, consisting for
the most part of hilly jungles, through which
roads had to be made as the force proceeded.
Then, too, the conditions of life were different
from those usual to a military camp, for as we
learn from an officer who has told the story of
the expedition at some length, the native
soldiers and camp coolies, on arriving at a
camping-ground, at once set to work cutting
the jungle and building " quarters." " In an
almost incredibly short space of time they ran
up quarters for the general and other officers
with him. The framework was fastened together by strips of bark, and the walls consisted
of bamboo, leaves, and grass. Each hut was
furnished with a standing bedstead, a table
and stool of bamboo. Outside was the mess-
table, the superstructure of which was formed
of split bamboo, supported by legs of rough
timber; and around it were seats constructed
also of split bamboo. It was astonishing how
soon a waste, howling wilderness of jungle was
transformed into a pleasant camp; and as
abundance of firewood was at hand, large
camp fires were always maintained, which

tended to keep these halting places drier and healthier than might have been expected."

An amusing example of mother wit *versus* science was afforded during this expedition. At one of the camping-grounds it was found necessary to utilise both sides of a stream, and " a light bridge was thrown across the Tapai by the Cachari Kookies. Practical fellows these, caring little for mathematics and theory. While a scientific officer was calculating, in a hut close by, the strength of timber necessary for the bridge, the weight of troops likely to pass over it, the force of the current and other considerations to which education and engineering books teach us to attach importance, as necessary to the safe construction of a bridge, these Kookies, who had never heard of Tredgold, and probably would not be any handier if they had, had actually built a bridge with the materials, small timber and bamboos, nearest to hand— a bridge built so substantially that it lasted throughout the campaign. When the aforesaid Engineer officer came out with his design and calculation—faultless, no doubt, in every detail—we may feel sure he looked rather surprised when he saw his work done for him." * Lord Roberts, too, tells the same amusing story in his recollections of this campaign in his " Forty-one Years in India."

Many difficulties were encountered in the progress of the column during November and December, and the Assistant-Quartermaster-General was kept incessantly busy exploring for available routes. On December 23rd it was determined to attack the Kholel village, and Roberts, well in front with the advance guard and ascending through a dense growth of jungle, had a preliminary brush with the enemy. The tribes did not make much of a stand at any point, but kept up a desultory firing on the advancing expedition. The Kholel villages were captured, and the firing was continued occasionally, but not with any serious effect. Indeed, Lieutenant Woodthorpe tells us that although the Lushais maintained their firing, yet on Christmas Day, "to keep up a semblance of the season," a big

* " The Lushai Expedition," by R. S. Woodthorpe, Lieut., R.E.

table was placed on a raised position out in the open, and all the officers of the expedition dined together. Despite the shots flying about, none of the officers were hit, and, curiously enough, while the singing which followed the "Christmas dinner" was going on, the enemy ceased firing, though they began again as soon as the singing ceased.

On January 1, 1872, while prosecuting this expedition, Colonel Roberts had a very agreeable New Year's gift in the form of news from headquarters that, a vacancy having occurred, he had been appointed Deputy-Quartermaster-General. A few days later, too, he received the gratifying intelligence of the birth of a son.

His duties as Quartermaster during the expedition were rendered the more difficult by the fact that the villagers, even where they were not actively militant, would not point out the way—or else would point out the wrong way, as they did on one occasion when Colonel Roberts felt convinced that there must be a more direct road, and was absolutely untiring in his endeavours to discover it, until

at length success rewarded his efforts. We
further learn that at one spot Roberts,
being well ahead of the column, at a sudden
turn in the road where it skirted a hill, came
in sight of a stockade built right across it at
a distance of a mile or so away. It would
have probably meant a severe loss to have
marched straight on the stockade, so the
resourceful officer made a detour "entailing
a long and weary drag up and down steep
spurs, at one time attaining a height of six
thousand feet, till at last he struck the road
again about a mile beyond the stockade,"
much, we may be sure, to the surprise and
discomfiture of the tribes.

At length the punitive expedition accomplished its purpose, the kidnapped girl, Mary
Winchester, had been given up to the other
column, and the troops returned to Calcutta
and were distributed to various centres. In
thanking the forces under him the General
said, "the history of the expedition from first
to last has been one of sheer hard work."

It is interesting to note that it was during
this expedition that Colonel Roberts picked

Photo by] [GLOVER, DUBLIN.

LORD ROBERTS AND HIS FAVOURITE CHARGER, "VONOLEL."

(*" Vonolel" is the white Arab upon which Lord Roberts rode during the Kabul-
Kandahar march. The charger was awarded a special decoration by
order of her Majesty.*)

up the name which he afterwards gave to his
celebrated white charger, Vonolel. This was
the name of one of the brave tribal leaders
whose grave was visited towards the end of
the long and trying march of the Lushai
Expedition.

D.Q.M.G. Colonel Roberts reached Simla on
April 1, 1872, exactly twenty years after he
had landed at Calcutta as a youthful cadet
fresh from Addiscombe. In the autumn, when
the list of honours awarded to those who
had distinguished themselves in the Lushai
expedition was published, Colonel Roberts
found himself gazetted a Companion of the
Bath.

For a few years there was peace in the
British dominions in Asia, and the time was
passed in the invaluable, if unobtrusive duties
of an officer of the headquarters staff during
the "piping times of peace." These duties
as Deputy-Quartermaster-General continued
from 1872 until 1875. At the end of January
of the last-named year Roberts was gazetted
a Brevet-Colonel, and was shortly after appointed to the chief position in the department

with which he had been so long identified, becoming Quartermaster-General.

It was, as many readers will recollect, in 1875 that the Prince of Wales made his tour through India, and Colonel Roberts' position made him responsible for many of the arrangements in the carrying out of the details of that historic progress. An interesting feature, for which the Quartermaster-General was entirely responsible, was the erection, when the Prince's camp occupied the famous Ridge at Delhi, of miniature embrasures showing the positions and objects of the breaching batteries which had done such fine service eighteen years earlier.

Within less than a year after the return of the Prince of Wales from the East, the Queen was proclaimed (on January 1, 1877) Empress of India, the proclamation being made with great ceremonial at Delhi. Again the Quartermaster-General had to undertake the formation of a great camp at the old Moghul capital, and to bear his part in one of the most brilliant ceremonials in the whole history of India. A large volume has been written on this Imperial assemblage, one passage from which will suggest the work which the organisers of the camp must have had to do: " The scene on the morning of the Proclamation (January 1, 1877) assumed a varied and dazzling character. Every ruling chief, and every European Governor and Lieutenant-Governor sat under his own banner, surrounded by native nobles and European officials. Every effort was made to mingle the ruling chiefs with European officials, so as to avoid questions of precedence, which have excited bitterness and heartburnings in India from the remotest antiquity. The result was such a display of Oriental costumes and insignia with British uniforms and banners as was never witnessed before. Sixty-three ruling chiefs of India were present in the amphitheatre. They and their retinues, all in gorgeous costumes of satin, velvet, or cloth of gold, were everywhere mixed up with European officials in their uniforms of red and dark blue."

In the following year Colonel Roberts, having completed his three years as Quarter-

9

master-General, was delighted to have the chance of a command, when the Viceroy (Lord Lytton) proposed to offer him a new post which was about to be created, that of Chief Commissioner of the North-west Frontier district. Before taking up the Chief Commissionership, however, he was appointed to the command of the Punjab Frontier Force. This Roberts took over in March, 1878, and having inspected all the posts held by the Frontier Force, returned to Simla in May to discuss with the Viceroy particulars of the proposed new Commissionership.

Events were moving rapidly towards the Afghan War, which was to considerably alter the ambitious officer's future, to make his name familiar as a household word in the mouths of his countrymen, and to show the world that in his person England had a really great military leader. That war and its events must claim our attention in another chapter.

CHAPTER VIII

TROUBLE between the Government of India and the Amir of Afghanistan had been brewing for some time, when, in the summer of 1878, Major Cavagnari, as forerunner of Sir Neville Chamberlain's mission, was stopped by an Afghan force and prevented from proceeding to Kabul. This insulting rebuff rendered war almost unavoidable; subsequent events made it inevitable. Into the merits of the quarrel between the two countries this is not the place to inquire. The course of the war interests us as showing the great qualities of the leader who, at first in command of the Kuram Field Force, and later, in

Afghanistan itself, was to give signal proofs of his capacity as a soldier and commander of soldiers.

In view of the threatening outlook, two columns were ordered to be formed, one for a possible advance in the direction of Kandahar, and the other for operating in the Kuram Valley. The command of the latter was given to Colonel Roberts, with of course the local rank of Major-General. Before he took up his duties at the headquarters of the Kuram Field Force at Kohat, a third column was ordered to be formed for use in the Khyber Pass district. The three columns as first planned aggregated nearly 36,000 men, but General Roberts' force had rather less than 5,000 of these, although after a few months it was brought up by reinforcements to something over 13,000.

Of the three lines of advance—from the Khyber, Kuram, and Quetta—the Government attached the greatest importance to the second —the column the story of which is here the most important one to us. As Lord Lytton, the Viceroy, said in one of his despatches:

" The Amir could scarcely fail to perceive that if he allowed a British force, advancing on this line, to reach the Shutargardan in full strength, both Kabul and Ghazni would remain completely at its mercy. It was therefore, probable that the strongest resistance to our advance would be made by his Highness at some point in the Upper Kuram Valley, where his troops would command positions of great strength easy to hold and very difficult to attack. It was equally probable that, if Sher Ali's army were thoroughly beaten here, its defeat would immediately be felt in the very heart of his power, which must be more severely shaken by the loss of a battle in the Kuram than by similar disaster in any other part of his dominions. Our object, therefore, in despatching a force to the Kuram, was to defeat and disperse any Afghan army which might be found there, and to seize with the utmost rapidity a position directly menacing Kabul and Ghazni, but without advancing beyond the Shutargardan."

The measures contemplated by the Indian

Government were—(1) The immediate issue of a manifesto which should define the cause of offence, declare a friendly disposition towards the Afghan people, and reluctance to interfere in their internal affairs, and should fix the whole responsibility of what might happen upon the Amir. (2) An advance into the Kuram Valley as soon as the force at Kohat was ready to move. (3) The expulsion of the Afghans holding the Khyber Pass. (4) An advance from Quetta into Pishin, or, if necessary, to Kandahar.

When General Roberts arrived at Kohat on October 9th and took over the command of the Kuram Field Force he had his first experience of independent leadership. During the quarter of a century in which he had been winning his way to that proud position he had had the distinction of being " mentioned in despatches " no fewer than twenty-three times. On the morrow of his arrival at Kohat the General ordered part of his force to begin the forward movement to a point near the frontier. Thence on November 21st the troops began crossing the frontier, General Roberts himself accompanying the advanced guard. The enemy vacated one or two mud-forts, which were successively occupied by the British forces, and retired towards the village of Peiwar and the Peiwar Kotal—a mountain ridge in which they could find strong natural positions. The occupation of these mud-forts was the gaining of the first objective point in the campaign, says its historian,* for " though they were practically useless for purposes of defence, [they] afforded all that was necessary in the way of accommodation and storage room at the outset. Afterwards they were found to be rather small, but at first they gave the security that was wanted, for the collection of the hospital, commissariat, engineer and ordnance park stores, that accompanied the force."

Rumours came to the General that the Afghans, in retiring on the Peiwar Kotal, were finding it necessary to abandon a number of guns, and a forward movement was at once decided upon, with the object, if possible, of capturing these. This led to one of the most

* Major J. A. S. Colquhoun's " With the Kurram Field Force, 1878-79."

brilliant events of General Roberts' campaign
in the Kuram Valley, the capture of a seemingly
impregnable position held by a strong body of
Afghan warriors. The news as to the abandoned guns proved to be untrue, as was discovered when the troops had advanced; and
after some desultory firing they retired to a
camping-ground in the valley which had been
found to be clear of the enemy. Just as the
camp equipment began to arrive an unpleasant
"hint" came from an Afghan gun nearly two
thousand yards away. The artillery was at
once brought into play, and replied, and under
cover of its fire the camp was shifted to a safer
place—no easy matter in a scrub-grown
country with dusk rapidly closing in. "Thus
ended the reconnaissance to the foot of the
Peiwar Kotal—an operation which has been
misconstrued by some as intending and
involving a direct attack on an almost impregnable position." The real attack itself
was to come four days later, and meanwhile
General Roberts was maturing his plans, and he
and his officers were reconnoitring alternative
routes. By December 1st these plans had

been formed, and on the following day the
General began to put them into execution.
His design was, while making a feint of attacking the position from the front, to really
deliver the main attack from a direction
where it had been found that "the features
of the ground rendered it much less strong
as a military position." The plan was to
make a night march, and arriving at the foot
of the Kotal by daybreak, to storm it and turn
the enemy's position.

It was dark though starlight at about ten
o'clock on the night of December 1st, when the
force began to move silently out of camp, with
this object of turning the Afghan position.
The camp fires were left burning brightly, that
the foe should have no inkling of the move that
was taking place. It was a slow and dangerous
march, and at about six o'clock the enemy
were first encountered, and after rather more
than an hour's stubborn fighting their first
position on the Spingawi plateau was occupied,
and General Roberts had the gratification of
finding the whole of the turning force and its
supports on the top of the mountain. After a

was no other weapon of offence or defence lying ready to his hand upon which he might count in case of need. Visions of a retreat to Kuram, or even to Thull, of harassing attacks from treacherous hill tribes, and possible mutinies in our rear . . . presented themselves unbidden to the mind."

The success was complete, the General's operations having been characterised by a "happy combination of prudence and audacity." From the beginning, as one of his subalterns on this occasion recorded, he had succeeded in inspiring all who were under his command—men and officers alike—with the most implicit confidence in his judgment as a skilful general and in his boldness as an intrepid leader. He took three or four days to mature his plans for attacking, but he utilised those days of healthful rest for his men in discovering all he could as to the possible routes for turning the Afghan position, and in arranging the details of the attack with such precision as is possible to a military commander. "When the moment for action arrived he was able to lead his troops during the dark midnight hours through formidable mountain defiles to the selected point of attack. Without serious pause or check he struck a succession of sudden and effectual blows. When the difficulty of the ground and the number of enemies arrested his advance, without wasting life in needless effort he suspended his attack, and guided by a sure *coup d'œil*, carried out the bold and skilful dispositions for seizing the line of the enemy's retreat, which decided the success of the day."

A few days after this fight General Roberts had the gratification of receiving from the Viceroy a message from the Queen, in which her Majesty said: "I have received the news of the decisive victory of General Roberts and the splendid behaviour of my brave soldiers with pride and satisfaction, though I must ever deplore the unavoidable loss of life. Pray inquire after the wounded in my name. May we continue to receive good news."

Besides reading to them the message from the Queen, the General in command issued

a congratulatory order in which he cordially
thanked the troops for the able way in which
they had aided him in winning the success.
This, the first order of its kind which he
issued, is well worth quoting : "Major-General
Roberts congratulates the Kuram Field Force
on the successful result of the operations of
the 2nd December against the Peiwar Kotal,
a position of extraordinary strength, and held
by an enemy resolute and well armed. Not
only had the enemy the advantage of ground,
but also of numbers, as they were largely reinforced from Kabul the evening previous to
the attack. A position apparently impregnable
has been gained. A considerable portion of
the Afghan army has been completely routed,
and seventeen guns, with large stores of
ammunition and supplies, have been captured.
The result is most honourable, and could only
have been achieved by troops in a high state
of discipline—capable of enduring hardships
—and able to fight as soldiers of the British
army have always fought. Major-General
Roberts deeply regrets the brave men who
have fallen in the gallant discharge of their

duty, and feels for the suffering of the wounded."

The triumph on the Peiwar Kotal was the principal event of the campaign, although the Kuram Field Force continued in the district for many months, during which time useful work was being done by the commander and those under him. One incident that followed on the capture of the Kotal calls for more particular mention as illustrating the firmness and decision of the General. During the night advance an incident occurred that might have jeopardised the success of the action and even the lives of all concerned in the flanking movement. Suddenly from the ranks of a native regiment at the head of the column the report of a rifle was heard, immediately followed by another. A native officer discovered which men had fired their rifles, but tried to screen his co-religionists. The incident was allowed to pass at the moment, the enemy, who might have been warned by the sound, seemingly not having noticed it ; but General Roberts was too good a commander to forget the episode, and before setting out on a reconnaissance to the Shutar-gardan Pass ordered a court of inquiry to be held at Alikhel, which he had made temp-orary headquarters, and to report to him on his return. Finally, a court-martial was held on the two men, on the officer who had condoned their offence, and on eighteen others who had left their regiment during the fight. The man who first fired his rifle was sentenced to death, and the others to varying terms of imprisonment—" a necessary, but most unpleasant, duty."

General Roberts made a reconnaissance to the top of the Shutargardan Pass, and gathered useful knowledge of that route to Kabul. He then set out with a small force to the Khost Valley, with the view of exploring that district and discovering its resources in men and supplies. Early in January, 1879, his force had some fighting, though there was no serious or sustained opposition to their investigations. Returning to his main camp, he saw his troops comfortably settled in their winter quarters, and then inspected the disposition of his forces from Peiwar Kotal to the base at

Kohat. Dr. Joshua Duke, of the Bengal Medical Service, who attended General Roberts throughout his subsequent Afghan campaign, has described arriving at the Kuram camp in the middle of March, in which we get a pleasant personal glimpse of the hero of the Peiwar Kotal: "Having warmed the inner man, and recovered from the fatigues of the journey, I proceeded to make some official visits in the headquarters camp, and saw General Roberts himself, who was kind enough to give me a glass of milk punch of the most excellent quality. A shaggy beard hid the lower part of his face, so that at first I hardly recognised him; but the old cheerful smile and kindly manner were unchanged."

Towards the end of March the Commander-in-Chief of the Forces in India (Sir Frederick Haines) visited Kuram and complimented General Roberts on the appearance of the troops, and expressed his satisfaction at meeting them in sight of the Peiwar Kotal, where their gallant action was fought. The Commander-in-Chief alluded to the remarkably good behaviour of the Kuram Field Force,

10

not an instance of any complaint as regards the behaviour of the men having been brought to his notice. At the same time he said that the other columns of the Kabul force had behaved equally well, and though they had not had the good luck which had fallen to the Kuram Field Force, yet they merited as much praise, as in no way was their conduct behind that of the Kuram troops.

The death of the Amir Sher Ali and the assumption of authority by Yakub Khan somewhat altered the complexion of affairs, and just when General Roberts was making the necessary preparations for the advance on Kabul, as soon as the winter should be over, came news of peace negotiations; then the news that a treaty of peace had been signed and that a British Mission—instead of a Field Force—was to proceed to the Afghan capital. The treaty gave the General a free hand in inspecting the tract of country in which he was—a tract of country which was newly put under the authority of the Indian Government—and in surveying some of the passes that led into Afghanistan.

Peace being assured, the General took leave of the Kuram Field Force and returned to Simla.

Before his return, however, he had a small part to play in an act which preceded the tragedy at Kabul, which was to plunge India and Afghanistan into war again. This was the accompanying, on his way towards the Afghan capital, of Sir Louis Cavagnari, Envoy and Plenipotentiary to his Highness the Amir of Kabul. The ill-fated Cavagnari and his escort arrived at Kuram in the middle of July, and General Roberts and a number of officers accompanied the Envoy almost to the summit of the Shutargardan Pass, where they had a farewell dinner, on the conclusion of which, as Lord Roberts has told us in his famous book, he found his mind too full of gloomy forebodings to allow of his proposing, as he should have done, the health of Cavagnari. The following morning the parties continued together to the Afghan camp, and then separated—for ever, Cavagnari and his escort proceeding, full of hope, to the place where they were to be murdered by fanatics within a few weeks, while Roberts and his companions returned to Kuram.

For his services in this, his first independent command, General Roberts was accorded the thanks of both Houses of Parliament and was made a Knight Commander of the Bath.

CHAPTER IX

Murder of Cavagnari at Kabul—Roberts' command of
the Kabul Field Force—The advance—A desperate
situation — Flight of the enemy — Unfounded
charges.

THERE was to be but a brief interval
between the giving up by General
Roberts of the command of the Kuram Field
Force on the Afghan borders and his appointment to the command of another force with
far sterner work before it in the same quarter
of Asia ; but meanwhile he had, as I have said,
returned for a time to Simla, where he was
requested by Lord Lytton to become a member of a Commission of Inquiry, which was
formed for the purpose of investigating matters
concerning the organisation and expenditure
of the Indian army.   It is interesting to
know that many items of the series of reforms

suggested by Sir Frederick Roberts were largely adopted, some of them forthwith, while others, though accepted in theory, were many years before they took shape in practice.

Sir Frederick Roberts was still at Simla, hoping soon to hear that the home Government had ratified the creation of the new post which he was to occupy, when events were rapidly moving in Kabul towards a tragic close—a close that was to have far-reaching effects. Sir Louis Cavagnari had reached Yakub Khan's capital on July 24th, and his letters and telegrams led to the belief that all was going well with him and his party, although there were not wanting incidents of a more or less suspicious character. "In none of his private letters or official diaries has Louis Cavagnari at any time expressed the slightest apprehension for his personal safety, or that of members of the Embassy." The last letter which he wrote to the Viceroy, Lord Lytton, was penned on August 30th, and in it he said, "I have nothing whatever to complain of on the part of the Amir or his ministers, though there are many matters

I wish I could influence him about. There is no doubt that his authority is weak throughout the whole of Afghanistan. This is not to be wondered at after the years of misrule and oppression on Sher Ali Khan's part. But if he keeps straight he will pull through it. . . . His conduct of foreign relations is all that could be desired. . . . I have no doubt that when disaffected persons see that they get no encouragement from us things will settle down; and if Yakub Khan will only adopt a little more conciliation, and show his subjects that he is not going to use *our safeguard* as a means of grinding them down, all will go well."

Alas! all did not go well, as poor Cavagnari was soon to learn. On September 2nd his last telegram concluded with the words, "All well." On the following day the Residency was attacked by the Afghan soldiers, the Amir, despite all his protestations, apparently not lifting a finger to assist the Ambassador, and in a few hours Sir Louis Cavagnari and every member of his Embassy was murdered! The news came as a shock to the whole world. From Kabul it first reached the political officer at Alikhel, who telegraphed to General Roberts at Simla, and Sir Frederick was roused in the early hours of September 5th by a messenger, who handed him a telegram, despatched the day before, which ran : " One Jelaladin Ghilzai, who says he is in Sir Louis Cavagnari's secret service, has arrived in hot haste from Kabul, and solemnly states that yesterday morning the Residency was attacked by three regiments, who had mutinied for their pay, they having guns, and being joined by a portion of six other regiments. The Embassy and escort were defending themselves when he left about noon yesterday. I hope to receive further news."

The terrible tidings had of course to be acted upon at once. Of the three columns which had been formed, that in the Kuram Valley was the only one available, and Roberts was ordered to return and take up his command, the Brigadier-General, who had been acting during his absence, being instructed to move troops forthwith to the Shutargardan Pass.

On receipt of the direful news in England the Government telegraphed: "The occupation of Kabul is a necessity, and the advance upon it should be immediate." General Roberts left Simla for the front on September 6th, having arranged with the Commander-in-Chief as to the reinforcements which were to be sent up to him. At the same time General Stewart, who had been in command of the Kandahar column of a year before, was ordered to re-occupy that city, which he was on the point of vacating, and a movable column was also formed for occupying the Khyber Pass.

"On the 11th of September, 1879, at 5 a.m., the Shutargardan Pass was occupied without a shot being fired." Sir Frederick Roberts, having pushed forward as rapidly as possible to Alikhel, sent forward all available troops and matured all transport and commissariat arrangements, delaying his own advance over the Shutargardan Pass as long as possible for politic reasons; realising that as soon as he took the command it might be a signal to the Afghans to rise and bar his way to Kabul. His force was a small one—under eight thousand—and he had to arrange for keeping open a line of communication of about a hundred and fifty miles, and therefore postponed taking his place at the head of the Kabul Field Force, as it was now called, until everything was ripe for its advance on the mud-built city whose name it bore. Meanwhile, letters passed between the Amir and the General; the Amir betraying woful inconsistency in his lying about the course of events.

The British camp had been pushed forward to Kushi, whither on September 27th came the Amir Yakub Khan. On the following day Sir Frederick Roberts arrived in the afternoon, having been delayed with his escort, happily a strong one, on the Shutargardan Pass, where they had been attacked by a body of two thousand Afghans, who had hoped to be able to cut off the General, but who had been put to flight * without their being able to do much damage.

* It is interesting to learn that one of the Generals now in command in South Africa, General Hector Macdonald, then a colour-sergeant, distinguished himself greatly in this brush with the enemy, and in consequence of his bravery then and shortly after, won for himself " promotion from the ranks."

General Roberts' Field Force Order, issued
to his troops on taking over the command, is
well worthy of reproduction even in this brief
survey of his career for its direct appeal not
only to the courage but also to the common-
sense of his troops. It runs as follows:—

" The Government of India having decided
that a force shall proceed with all possible
despatch to Kabul, in response to his Highness the Amir's appeal for aid, and with the
object of avenging the dastardly murder of the
British representative and his escort, Sir
Frederick Roberts feels sure that the troops
under his command will respond to the call
with a determination to prove themselves
worthy of the high reputation they have maintained during the recent campaign.

" The Major-General need address no words
of exhortation to soldiers whose courage and
fortitude have been so well proved. The
Afghan tribes are numerous, but without
organisation; the regular army is undisci-
plined, and whatever may be the disparity in
numbers, such foes can never be formidable
to British troops. The dictates of humanity

require that a distinction should be made between the peaceable inhabitants of Afghanistan and the treacherous murderers for whom a just retribution is in store, and Sir Frederick Roberts desires to impress upon all ranks the necessity for treating the unoffending population with justice, forbearance, and clemency.

"The future comfort and well-being of the force depend largely on the friendliness of our relations with the districts from which supplies must be drawn; prompt payment is enjoined for all articles purchased by departments and individuals, and all disputes must be at once referred to a political officer for decision.

"The Major-General confidently looks forward to the successful accomplishment of the expedition, and the establishment of order and a settled Government in Afghanistan."

On October 2nd the general advance from Kushi took place, the Amir accompanying Sir Frederick Roberts. The General, being possessed of the full powers of our late plenipotentiary as well as his military position, "was a greater man than formerly, and a guard of honour of the 92nd Highlanders,

under a European officer, watched over his tent
in addition to the Gurkha guard, a stalwart
Gordon Highlander pacing in front while a
sturdy Nepaul Highlander stood sentinel in the
rear." Thus the force proceeded with but
little molestation to within a few miles of
Kabul, when there was a severe encounter,
which, however, proved a triumphant victory
for General Roberts. In but little more than
a month after he had left Simla he, to use the
words of the Viceroy, "made his triumphal
entry into Kabul at the head of as fine a force
as was ever put into the field, after having
given the Afghans a severe thrashing at
Charasiab, and captured two of their standards
and one hundred and fifty of their guns without the loss of a single officer."

On reaching Kabul General Roberts made a
public proclamation, announcing the reasons
for the presence there of his army, and the
intentions of the British Government. He had
been given very comprehensive instructions,
although at the same time very full independent powers, as may be gathered from the
following passages from the despatch conveying

those instructions : " In regard to the punishment of individuals, it should be swift, stern,
and impressive, without being indiscriminate
or immoderate; its infliction must not be
delegated to subordinate officers of minor
responsibility, acting independently of your
instructions or supervision; and you cannot
too vigilantly maintain the discipline of the
troops under your orders, or superintend their
treatment of the unarmed population, so long
as your orders are obeyed and your authority
is unresisted. You will deal summarily in the
majority of cases with persons whose share in
the murder of anyone belonging to the British
Embassy shall have been proved by your
investigations, but while the execution of
justice should be as public and striking as
possible, it should be completed with all
possible expedition, since the indefinite pro-
longation of your proceedings might spread
abroad unfounded alarms. . . . It will probably
be essential, not only for the protection of
your own camp from annoyance, but also for
the security of the well-affected population,
and for the general maintenance of order, that

you should assume and exercise supreme authority in Kabul, since events have unfortunately proved that the Amir has lost that authority, or that he has conspicuously failed to make use of it."

This was only the second occasion on which Sir Frederick Roberts held a general's command, but his instructions showed the implicit confidence which the Government reposed in him. His position was rendered trebly difficult by the fact of his holding political and diplomatic powers; however, he hoped, and not without reason, that "common sense and a sense of justice" would see him safely through.

Shortly after his occupation of Kabul he received a despatch giving him the local rank of Lieutenant-General and full command of all the troops in Eastern Afghanistan—numbering in the aggregate about 20,000 men.

During October and November there was much to be done, not only in the way of bringing to justice those responsible for the murder of Cavagnari and his staff, but in keeping order in the city and in arranging fitting quarters for the army during the approaching winter. But though the weeks passed quietly there were not wanting signs of approaching trouble. A fanatic priest, Mushk-i-Alam, started preaching a "holy war" against the Christian invaders and their allies, while a growing menace to General Roberts' army was the ever-increasing number of regular Afghan troops which, without pay or employment, but with arms and ammunition, began to return from various places to the neighbourhood of the capital.

The British and Indian forces were encamped in the Sherpur Cantonment—a great enclosure at the foot of a range of low hills, four miles long, about two miles from the nearest Kabul gate.

By the first week in December the situation began to get somewhat threatening, and on the 7th Sir Frederick Roberts telegraphed: "Affairs round Kabul less satisfactory of late. In Maidan, Sirdar Mahomed Hussain Khan has been murdered, apparently by men of Mushk-i-Alam's rising. Sirdar Abdullah Khan has been attacked by armed bands

in Logar, and for a time besieged in a
fort. Some Kohistani Maliks have come in,
but the leading man sends excuses, and the
country is reported very unquiet. . . . Anxious
as I am to avoid further expeditions at present, I may be forced, if this movement
spreads, to send out troops again."

Despite the anxiety of the situation the
officers and men treated the rumour with
outward indifference, and " on the 6th of
December a large picnic was given by the
General near Babar Badshah's tomb, on the
left of the Deh Mazung gorge, to which all
officers were invited, with their knives and
forks. After the picnic there was a paper-
chase, which finished up near the ground over
which our cavalry were to charge so des-
perately a few days afterwards. This chase
was celebrated for the number of falls which
happened, owing to the difficult nature of the
ditches, the banks of which were lined with
willows and poplars whose branches whisked
off several riders. Upwards of half the field
were unhorsed, many more than once. Even
our gallant General, who was well mounted,

11

showed the mark of Mother Earth on his coat.
General Dand Shah, then a guest, followed
the chase in his way, and appeared thoroughly
to enjoy it. The hares on this memorable
occasion were a captain of the 9th Lancers,
and a heavy-weight belonging to the Rifle
Brigade.

"Our last peaceful act took place on the 8th
of December, when a parade of all the troops
in Sherpur was held on the Behmaru plain, to
present distinguished-conduct medals to men
of the 72nd Highlanders as well as to show
the people who attended our teeth and our
mettle." °

The change was not long in coming, and
General Roberts' army was soon fighting not
only for the retention of Kabul but also for its
very existence. On December 11th a very
threatening situation arose, through two
columns sent out against the enemy failing to
effect an arranged junction, but the day was
saved by the coolness and bravery of General
Roberts, who managed a retirement from a

* Dr. Joshua Duke's "Recollections of the Kabul
Campaign, 1879 and 1880."

very dangerous position. It is as essential for a good commander to know when to retire as it is for him to know when to strike, and it was only when the case was desperate that General Roberts, who had come up just in time, gave the orders to the gunners to cut the traces and gallop off, thus avoiding the useless sacrifice of many valuable lives. For four days the fighting went on with fanatical zeal on one side and dogged bravery on the other, but the result of the fighting on December 14th was such that General Roberts ordered the concentration of all his forces within the Sherpur Cantonments—"a weaker man might have ruined us with half measures." His fighting force there numbered but about 5,000 men. There were many excursions and alarums during the following ten days, the Afghans making a great show of attacking Sherpur but without any serious loss to the Kabul Field Force. On December 23rd a very fierce attack on the Cantonment was made by the enemy, who had been persuaded by their leaders that the British troops had deserted. It was said that all the officers had ridden away from Sherpur, because some cavalry had cut its way through to communicate with reinforcements on their way. The enemy were further inspirited to this last suicidal attack by the report that most of General Roberts' troops had been killed and that the Cantonment walls were "manned" "mainly by goats with turbans artfully arranged on their heads!"

At length, after this big demonstration on the 23rd, they gave up the attempt. "On the following morning it was soon noised abroad that the Afghan army had bolted, and that during the night the many thousands collected to drive us out of the country had melted imperceptibly away." This result was partly owing to the unflinching stand made by General Roberts' gallant little army and partly to the fact being known that reinforcements were at hand.

The holding of the Cantonment in the face of great numbers of the enemy was especially creditable not only for the fighting but for the completeness of the arrangements which had been made for feeding the army. Before

SIR FREDERICK ROBERTS READING A PROCLAMATION TO THE CITY OF KABUL.

getting entirely cut off from the outer world
General Roberts had managed to procure pro-
visions for about four months, to say nothing
of provender for the horses and baggage
animals. It must be remembered, too, that
it was bad winter weather at the time. As
General Roberts himself said, "I think I had
great reason to be proud of my force. All
night and every night, the ground covered
with snow and the thermometer marking
sixteen degrees of frost, officers and men are
at their posts, and each day every available
man had to be hard at work strengthening the
defences. Native and European soldiers alike
bore the hardships and the exposure with the
utmost cheerfulness, and in perfect confidence
that, when the assault should take place,
victory would be ours."

Immediately after the disappearance of the
enemy General Roberts issued a proclamation,
saying, "At the instigation of some seditious
men, the ignorant people, generally not considering the result, raised a rebellion. Now
many of the insurgents have received their
reward, and as subjects are a trust from God,

the British Government, which is just and merciful, as well as strong, has forgiven their guilt." General pardon was offered to all who came in without delay, excepting, of course, certain ringleaders, and the result of the proclamation was the early restoration of quiet in the city. Afterwards the time passed rapidly in the completing of the clearance of the ground all round Sherpur, in the maintenance of order in the mud-built city of Kabul, and in the strengthening of existing defences and the erection of others in case of any fresh trouble arising.

The change must have been a welcome one to everybody there, but most of all to Sir Frederick Roberts, who had fully recognised from the first the enormous difficulties of the position. How the renewed freedom struck some of the officers of the Force may be gathered from the following note written by one of their number: " Building of men's and officers' quarters was again commenced. Messhouses rapidly showed themselves. The line of communication was reopened, and the post arrived with regularity. Adventurous Parsee

and Mahommedan merchants began to come
up from India, some of whom made large
profits. Beer on its first arrival sold at four
rupees a bottle, nearly eight shillings, and
other articles were at first equally dear."

The early part of 1880 thus sped away, and
in April the Government determined to send
a large force from Kandahar to Kabul under
the command of General Sir Donald Stewart.
The reason for this may best be stated in a
summary of an official minute on the subject
made by the Viceroy :—

"The Government is anxious to withdraw as
soon as possible the troops from Kabul, and
from all points beyond those to be occupied
under the Treaty of Gandamak, except Kandahar. In order that this may be done, it is
desirable to find a ruler for Kabul, which will
be separated from Kandahar. Steps are being
taken for this purpose. Meanwhile it is essential that we should make such a display of
strength in Afghanistan as will show that we
are masters of the situation, and will overawe
disaffection. But it is not desirable to spread
our troops over a large tract of country, or to

send small columns to any place where they would encounter opposition and increase the hostile feeling against us. All that is necessary, from the political point of view, is for General Stewart to march to Ghazni, break up any opposition he may find there or in the neighbourhood, and open up direct communication with Sir F. Roberts at Kabul. This he can do either by the direct route or by Kushi, as he may think to be most expedient under such conditions as may exist when he is at Ghazni."

On March 30th Sir Donald Stewart set out with his force from Kandahar, and having fought a big battle at Ghazni, he reached Kabul on May 5th, and, being the senior officer, took over the supreme command of the united forces. The day was not a very cheering one for General Roberts, for, besides having to hand over his command, he learned of the change of Ministry in England—with a probable change of policy in the East—and also of the resignation of Lord Lytton, the Viceroy, for whom he had established a very warm feeling of friendship.

The united forces were known as the Northern Afghanistan Field Force, and it was divided into three divisions, of two of which Sir Frederick Roberts himself retained command. For several months he had a quiet time, taking a few weeks of necessary rest by accompanying a brigade which was being sent to a distance.

Things in Afghanistan seemed at length to be shaping towards a fairly satisfactory close. The English Government was supporting the claim of Abdur Rahman to be Amir, provided that he would agree to certain stipulated conditions. Meanwhile Ayub Khan, a brother of the ex-Amir, Yakub Khan, was forming a large army to support his pretensions. Yakub Khan, on his resignation, had been despatched to India, where he was kept in virtual imprisonment for his connection with the massacre of the British Embassy.

During the progress of the Kabul Campaign several lightly made but very serious charges directed against General Roberts' army were repeated in England. It was said that cruelty was practised on the Afghan prisoners, that some of these were shot and others burnt, and so on. When he heard of these charges General Roberts sent a spirited and categorical denial in a letter of some length, which was read in the House of Lords by Viscount Cranbrook on February 13, 1880. In remarking that he had not refused to allow civilian newspaper correspondents to accompany the Kabul Field Force, the General had a neat hit at some of them, saying, "They are allowed to send any telegram they please, even when the information in them is incorrect."

CHAPTER X

TO the soldier his opportunities of distin-
guishing himself come with unexpected
suddenness, and it certainly was so in the case
of General Roberts. After his long service as
a staff officer, he got unexpectedly the appointment to the command of the Kuram Field
Force. He won such distinction by his
courageous and brilliant capture of the Peiwar
Kotal that he was no doubt at once marked for
future service when occasion should arise. In
the intercourse of State with State such
occasion might not have arisen for many years,
but as things happened within a few months
his services were again called into requisition

by the necessity of occupying Kabul after the
murder of Sir Louis Cavagnari. In the
summer of 1880 this service seemed within
measurable distance of being at an end, and
arrangements were even being made for the
withdrawal of the divisions which he commanded from Kabul back to India, when an
incident occurred which changed his future
and brought out in striking relief his qualities
as leader of a difficult expedition.

Before beginning the retirement of his
divisions *viâ* the Kuram route, by which he
had entered Afghanistan, Sir Frederick
Roberts set out to see something of the Khyber
route; visited Gandamak and Jalalabad, and
then suddenly, for no namable reason, the
officer gave up his tour and hurried back to
Kabul, prompted merely by "a presentiment
of coming trouble which I can only characterise
as instinctive." The trouble was only too
certain. Before he reached Kabul General
Roberts met Sir Donald Stewart, and heard
from him of the disaster at Maiwand, where,
of a force of 2,476 men engaged, no fewer
than 934 had been killed in a battle with

Ayub Khan. This disaster caused a crisis in our affairs in Afghanistan, and rendered the position of the garrison in Kandahar a precarious one. That city was hemmed in by a vast Afghan army flushed with its great success over General Burrows' Brigade, and it was vitally necessary to the maintenance of British prestige, not only in that country but probably in India also, that Kandahar should be relieved as rapidly and as effectually as possible. Sir Frederick Roberts at once conceived the idea of proceeding to Kandahar with a column to consist of troops who had been engaged in the Kabul Field Force, and, with the consent of Sir Donald Stewart, on July 30th despatched the following telegraphic message to the Adjutant-General of India at Simla :—

"Personal and secret. I strongly recommend that a force be sent from this to Kandahar. Stewart has organised a very complete one consisting of nine regiments of infantry, three of cavalry, and three mountain batteries. This will suffice to overcome all opposition *en route*, it will have the best possible effect on the country, and will be ready to go anywhere on reaching

Kandahar, being fully equipped in all respects.
He proposes sending me in command.

"I am sure that but few Bombay regiments
are able to cope with Afghans, and once the
Kabul Field Force leaves this country, the
chance of sending a thoroughly reliable and
well-equipped column will be lost. The movement of the remainder of the Kabul troops
towards India should be simultaneous with the
advance of my division towards Kandahar, it
being most desirable to limit the area of our
responsibilities as soon as possible; at the
same time it is imperative that we should now
show our strength throughout Afghanistan.
The withdrawal, under existing circumstances,
of the whole force from Kabul to India would
certainly be misunderstood, both in Afghanistan and elsewhere. You need have no fears
about my division. It can take care of itself,
and will reach Kandahar under the month.
I will answer for the loyalty and good feeling
of the native portion, and would propose to
inform them that, as soon as matters have
been satisfactorily settled at Kandahar, they
will be sent straight back to India. Show this
to Lyall."

On August 3rd came the welcome reply authorising the formation of the Kabul-Kandahar Field Force, with Sir Frederick Roberts in command. Sir Donald Stewart gave his friend a free hand in drawing upon the forces at Kabul, and General Roberts soon had at his disposal an army consisting of close upon 10,000 men of all ranks, and eighteen guns. This army was divided into three brigades of infantry and one of cavalry, and three mountain batteries of artillery. In addition there were just over 8,000 camp-followers and 2,300 horses and gun mules. All equipment was cut down to the very minimum so that the force might press forward with the very least hindrance, General Roberts even refusing to take with him any wheeled guns because of the necessary slowness in moving them, and so limiting himself to mountain batteries, the guns of which were carried on mules.

Says Dr. Duke of the start from Kabul : "At the mess table, the battle of Maiwand, with the terrible slaughter of our troops was, of course, much discussed, as well as its con-

sequences. Would the diminished garrison of
Kandahar be able to hold its own until our
arrival? Ayub Khan's great strength in
artillery, and the way he had used it, made
him seem a somewhat dangerous foe. The
rumour that Russian guidance was with them
was duly weighed; while the report that his
army was accompanied by 3,000 Turcoman
Horse, as they were called, raised the hope
that at last our cavalry might meet a foe
worthy of its steel. What lay before us could
not be foretold. At least the tiring monotony
of ordinary camp-life—for most of us hated
Kabul, Afghanistan, and Afghans generally—
was now to be changed, and war was in the
air. The march of General Roberts' division
to Kandahar caused no alteration of the
original intention of our Government to
vacate Afghanistan after the instalment of the
new Amir, Abdur Rahman. Two days after
our departure, General Sir Donald Stewart's
division marched for India. Sir F. Roberts'
army was then cut off from all communication
with India and the outer world. This fact
added, perhaps, a touch of seriousness to the

letters which, no doubt, most of us wrote the day before leaving Kabul, and invested the march with such intense interest to the general public."

This isolation of the force did certainly heighten the public interest in the great march which has given the General in command an undying fame. It may be recalled in his favour that at setting out General Roberts had to select from, in the army at Kabul, "the flower of the British regiments in India, as well as the crack regiments of the native army."

On August 3rd, as I have said, General Roberts received the telegram entrusting him with the formation and command of the Kabul-Kandahar Field Force; on August 7th the brigades to be employed, with everything cut down to its minimum, were ready for the start, which was begun early on the morning of the following day. General Roberts himself started two or three days later and caught up with the advance-guard of his little army on August 13th at Takin. On the following day they reached Ghazni, the scene of Sir

12

Donald Stewart's battle during his journey from Kandahar to Kabul four months earlier.

Some vivid idea of the difficulties of this portion of the trying march may be gathered from the account of it written by Lieutenant C. G. Robertson, to whose small volume I have before referred : " The dead pull," says that officer, " did not make itself felt till we left Saidabad in the Maidan Valley. From this point we said goodbye to all trees and verdure of every kind. Time seemed to resolve itself into an endless, scorching Indian day. Man and beast struggled on as if driven by an implacable fate. Under foot were stone and sand and choking dust ; on either hand a barren mountain wall neither closing in nor opening out ; and above and below and all around the dead, midday glare, seeming to dry up the marrow in your bones and make your soul faint within you. If shadows could have been made saleable, and rolled up in a commodious fashion, they would have fetched any price. Even the patch of shade under a horse's girth would have been a marketable object. I remember one day coming upon a ravine, where it was just possible to get a little shelter by sitting bolt upright against a bank of moist clay. An English officer, a little donkey, and a low-caste native had taken refuge there. I took my place among them with satisfaction. The amount of dirt it was possible to carry about on your person was positively startling. Getting into camp, I have a distinct recollection of often staring with wild, bloodshot eyes at myself and finding my features coated with dust past recognition. But the worst torment that pursued us was unquenchable thirst. Lips and throat were parched beyond the power of beakers of water to cool; and Tantalous-like dreams of impossible draughts of ruby-coloured claret-cup, or amber cider used to haunt my imagination till I thought I must drink something or perish."

The whole distance to be traversed was 320 miles, and as we have seen General Roberts undertook to cover this with his army, and all its essential equipment, in a month. How he succeeded the sequel will show. It may, however, be interesting to note from the record of one who accom-

panied the force, how he seasoned his men
to long and trying marches by more or less
closely alternating long and short ones. For
example, on the first day the army marched
eight miles, on the second ten, on the third
nineteen, and then eight, eighteen, eight,
fifteen, and fourteen—thus covering one hundred miles during the first eight days, or an
average of twelve and a half miles a day—an
average which was increased five-and-twenty
per cent. by the time the whole journey was
completed.

The progress of the Kabul-Kandahar Field
Force became the more trying the further
it proceeded on its way. Each day seemed
hotter and more wearisome than the preceding
ones after leaving Ghazni, for each day's march
meant a further descent towards the plains.
Little water, too, was obtainable at some points,
which of course helped seriously to hamper the
progress, for a long march can but badly be
borne by man or beast when water is not to be
had frequently. Still the cry was "On!" and
officers and men all worked with a will towards
the desired end. General Roberts himself was

indefatigable not only in getting the best work out of his troops, but also in looking, to the very best of his ability, after the comfort and well-being of the individuals composing the army which he was commanding on this somewhat hazardous enterprise. At the close of each day's march Sir Frederick Roberts himself saw the arrival of the very last part of the force before he retired to his tent for a brief rest. He learned the happy art of being able to snatch refreshing sleep in the shortest snatches. Much of the provision for the force had to be collected *en route*, either from the country passed directly through or from outlying villages, to which foraging excursions had to be made. All corn and other things taken from the villagers were strictly paid for in accordance with the order which I quoted in an earlier page.

On August 21st communication was opened by heliographic signalling with a point over thirty miles ahead, from which General Roberts learned news which made it necessary that every nerve should be strained to reach Kandahar at the earliest possible date. The news was of a disastrous *sortie* made by the garrison five days earlier, a disaster which meant so serious a loss that the surmise very naturally arose that the state of the garrison was so desperate as to necessitate desperate measures. On August 23rd the advanced guard reached Kelat-i-Gilzai, the point from which the signalling had been carried on two days earlier, and where there was a small garrison under Colonel Oriel Tanner. This force joined that of General Roberts, the fortress being abandoned. On August 24th the General gave his force a day's rest, which was especially needed by the transport animals and the doolie-bearers, whose work was probably severer than that of any other of the camp-followers.

The heat is said to have become more intolerable the nearer the little army got to its destination, but the hardened troops marched splendidly along. On the 26th two regiments of cavalry—the 3rd Punjab and the 3rd Bengal—received orders to be ready to march at midnight to Robat, over thirty-four miles away and within twenty miles of the besieged city, the object being to get into direct heliographic communication with Kandahar. The long march proved a terribly trying one, but its end was attained, and the besieged and relieving forces were soon "talking" to one another by means of the sun's rays. Ayub Khan was reported to be still at hand among the hills a couple of miles to the north of Kandahar. "This was good news for all. General Roberts was thus in direct communication and conversation with Kandahar on the twentieth day after his leaving Kabul, the distance accomplished in this time being just over 300 miles. Had it been advisable, or had there been any urgent necessity, our two cavalry regiments with their baggage might have reached Kandahar itself (318 miles) on the twenty-first day."

Another day's halt was given to all brigades on August 29th, and on the last day of the month the Kabul-Kandahar Field Force had, thanks to its plucky organiser, achieved a task which many persons considered an impossibility, a task the performance of which forms one of the most inspiriting chapters in our military annals. General Roberts, in his telegram to the Adjutant-General, had said that he could reach Kandahar in something less than a month, and magnificently did he keep his promise. The great march was his own idea; he organised the force and he worked with unfailing courage to the attainment of its end. As Dr. Duke has said in the book from which I have already quoted: "While it must be allowed that the whole force, men and officers, had done their duty nobly, and had accomplished a march which has seldom been surpassed, still the key of the movement was the firm determination of the General commanding. Few commanders have been more personally liked by all, from the drummer to the colonel, than was General Roberts; and the national and universal admiration which this march and subsequent complete victory inspired has stamped it as one of the greatest achievements of the British army."

Such was the tribute of one officer, an officer who accompanied the cavalry brigade on the historic march; but before describing the great victory over Ayub Khan's forces, which was the immediate and fitting sequel to the march, it may not be inappropriate to quote also a tribute from an officer who had not the good fortune to be mounted and who has recorded: " As one who took part in the march, and actually walked the whole distance, I can safely say it was extremely hard work, and could not possibly have been done except under a general like Sir Frederick Roberts, who was believed in and trusted by all ranks, and who inspired a determination to fall down rather than give in. The hardest marches were from Ghazni to Yarghati, the last three hours of which were through a blinding duststorm; from Mukur to Punjak (19 miles), a march without any water, except one muddy stream, the whole distance; and from Kheli-Akhund to Robat, the weather on this day being like an Indian hot-weather day. There were few serious cases of illness amongst the European troops, but much footsoreness; donkeys were bought in large numbers, on which the footsore men were placed. After Kelat-i-Ghilzai everyone suffered from diarrhœa. This, added to poor food, reduced the men so that I do not think the force

could have marched much further than it did.
Amongst the native soldiers were a few deaths,
and the mortality amongst the camp-followers
was much greater than was generally known.
The work on the ranks was excessive. Every
man in my batta was, if not on 'picquet,' on
some 'fatigue' every day, either before starting in the morning or after arrival in camp.
The chief cause of fatigue, however, was want
of sleep. The force generally marched so
early in the morning, and rear-guards got in
so late, that men on this latter duty obtained
very few hours' rest. I consider it was simply
the pluck of the men, inspired by the General's
presence and encouragement, that pulled the
force through."

For the last four days of the march General
Roberts was attacked by fever, and was compelled to give in for a time, and to allow
himself to be carried in a doolie, though he
was sufficiently recovered to be able to insist
upon mounting his charger for the meeting
with the Kandahar officers. Anticipating
that the Afghan general would make a stand,
General Roberts made but short marches on

the last two days, to allow of his troops
arriving in a fairly fresh condition, prepared
for any emergency.

As supplement to the plan of the route from
Kabul to Kandahar, given on next page, it
may be of interest, before touching upon
the subsequent battle, to give roughly the
distances marched on the different days :—

						MILES.
Aug.	8	Bala Hissar (Kabul) to Charasiab				8
,,	9	to Zahidabad	...	...	...	10
,,	10	,, Wazir Killa	...	...	...	19
,,	11	,, Baraki Barak ...	...	...	8
,,	12	,, Saidabad	...	...	...	18
,,	13	,, Takia ...	...	...	...	8
,,	14	,, Shasgao	...	...	...	15
,,	15	,, Ghazni	...	...	...	14
,,	16	,, Yarghati	...	...	...	17
,,	17	,, Chardeh	...	...	...	16
,,	18	,, Karez-i-Obah ...	...	...	15
,,	19	,, Mukur ...	...	...	...	19
,,	20	,, Punjak	...	...	...	19
,,	21	,, Gajon ...	...	...	...	16
,,	22	,, Baba Kazai	...	...	...	17
,,	23	,, Kelat-i-Ghilzai	...	...	17
,,	24	(A day's halt) ...	...	...	—
,,	25	,, Julduk...	...	...	...	15
,,	26	,, Tirandez (Minar)	...	...	14½
,,	27	,, Shahr-i-Safa (Mound) (cavalry reached Robat)		...	...	12
,,	28	,, Robat (infantry)	...	...	22½
,,	29	(A day's halt) ...	...	...	—
,,	30	,, Momand	...	...	...	7
,,	31	,, Kandahar (cantonment)	...	...	13

320

KABUL TO KANDAHAR

Sir F. Roberts' Stages
Sir D. Stewart's Stages

Scale of Miles.

PLAN OF GENERAL ROBERTS' MARCH FROM KABUL TO KANDAHAR.

On his arrival at Kandahar, in obedience with instructions from Simla, Sir Frederick Roberts assumed command of the forces in southern Afghanistan, and on the very day of his arrival ordered a reconnaissance to be made with the object of finding out the enemy's strength and dispositions. The Afghans attacked the reconnoitring troops, who retired, leaving Ayub Khan with the idea that he had scored another and an easy victory. His jubilation was premature and short-lived. General Roberts had learned from the reconnaissance all that he had wished to learn, and at once matured his plans for attacking the Afghan camp before the elated troops of Ayub Khan could have a chance of again attacking Kandahar. At six o'clock on the morning of September 1st the General summoned the commanding officers to him and explained his plan of operations. This plan was to threaten the enemy's centre and left in the Baba Wali Pass, while the real attack was made on the enemy's right, the cavalry being sent to threaten the enemy's flank and to cut off his line of retreat.

The plans were carried out in a perfect manner, the fighting being most severe, but resulting in a very complete victory for General Roberts' troops after a sustained and deadly artillery duel. The infantry rushed on the positions and drove the enemy off at the point of the bayonet, losing heavily but doing great damage on the enemy, and causing the Afghan leader to flee precipitately with the remnant of his army. Many deeds of heroism were performed on this day, both by men and officers who fell on the field of battle, and by others who lived to wear their justly earned honours. Among the latter I may mention Major White, of the 92nd Highlanders (now General Sir George White, the gallant defender of Ladysmith), who, when it became necessary to take the Baba Wali Kotal by storm, called upon his men for just one more charge " to close the business," dashed forward and was the first to reach the spot, closely followed by his men, who drove the enemy from their entrenchments at the point of the bayonet and captured the guns.

Throughout the long and memorable day

A CHARGE OF THE HIGHLANDERS IN THE BATTLE OF BABA WALI.

General Roberts had been hard at work direct-
ing the operations, despite the fact that, as I
have said, he had been so ill during the last
few days of the march that he had had to
be carried. To use his own words : "Utterly
exhausted as I was from the hard day's work
and the weakening effect of my late illness,
the cheers with which I was greeted by the
troops as I rode into Ayub Khan's camp and
viewed the dead bodies of my gallant soldiers
nearly unmanned me, and it was with a very
big lump in my throat that I managed to say
a few words of thanks to each corps in turn.
When I returned to Kandahar and threw
myself on the bed in the little room prepared
for me, I was dead beat and quite unequal to
the effort of reporting our success to the Queen
or to the Viceroy."* After an hour's rest the
indefatigable commander "pulled himself
together" and telegraphed his despatch. The
next morning it must indeed have been a
source of much gratification to him to have
realised all that he had done within one month
of receiving his orders at Kabul.

* Lord Roberts' "Forty-one Years in India."

Arrangements were at once made for sending the troops of the Kabul force back to India,
and before the end of September the last
brigade of the victorious Kabul army was on
its way thither.   General Roberts having been
requested to retain the command at Kandahar
until some definite arrangement was made,
proceeded to Quetta in the hope that a change
of climate might prove sufficiently beneficial
to permit of his continuing the command, but
after a few weeks he felt compelled to resign,
and started for India on October 12th.

For his great services in Afghanistan Sir
Frederick Roberts was made a G.C.B. and
appointed Commander-in-Chief of the Madras
army.

Before taking leave of this subject it will
not be inappropriate to quote, from a speech
which General Roberts delivered in England
a few months later, a passage on the subject
of the troops with which he had carried out
his signally successful operations.   He was
criticising the " short-service system," and
said : " The 72nd Highlanders continued with
me throughout the campaign, and was one of

the three battalions of British infantry I
selected to accompany me on the march from
Kabul to Kandahar. During the early part
of last spring the regiment had received a
draft from England of about 170 men.
While on the march to Kandahar I made
it my business to find out every day how
many men of each corps had fallen out on
the way. This information was necessary to
enable me to judge whether the troops were
being taxed beyond their powers. I discovered
that the 72nd Highlanders had more casualties
in proportion to their numbers than either the
60th Rifles or 92nd Highlanders; and, on
further inquiry, I ascertained that the majority
of the cases occurred among the men of the
last draft—in fact, among the young soldiers.
The average service of the 72nd Highlanders,
on our leaving Kabul, was: sergeants, 13½
years; corporals, 12½ years; privates, 7 years;
and of the 92nd Highlanders: sergeants,
15 years; corporals, 11 years; privates, 9
years. . . . Such a return as this it will be
quite impossible ever to prepare again if our
system of short service is persisted in, and

13

let me add something more, it will be as impossible for a British force ever again to perform such a march as those magnificent troops I had the honour and pride to command made from Kabul to Kandahar. No commander would venture to undertake such a service except with soldiers on whose discipline, spirit, and endurance, he could thoroughly rely. I never for a moment had a doubt as to the result; but then I had tried men, not untried and untrained boys, to depend upon." *

* Speech at the Mansion House, February 14, 1881.

CHAPTER XI

GENERAL ROBERTS himself thinks
that his command of the little army
that he took from Kuram to Kabul was a
more arduous undertaking than the march
which will be ever associated with his name;
his countrymen, impressed no doubt by the
" glamour of romance " thrown over the march
by its conditions, have always laid most stress
upon it, and when the " Hero of Kandahar "
returned to England on leave, as he did shortly
after leaving Afghanistan, he was fêted and
honoured on all hands. He landed at Dover
on November 17th, and the enthusiastic

reception which was then accorded to him
was but the prelude of a long series of
banquetings and other fêtes in his honour.
Happily he found his wife and his three
children well, though his country claimed so
much of him as the hero of the hour that it
is to be feared his experience of home life was
sadly cut up. It is not possible in this short
account of his life to name the many occasions
on which he was present as the honoured guest;
one or two instances must suffice as examples
of the whole. Dublin University gave him
the honorary degree of LL.D., and Oxford
followed with its D.C.L. At the end of
January he was presented with a handsome
service of plate at Bristol, a city in the
neighbourhood of which, as he said, his family
had resided for upwards of seventy years.
Wherever he went he had to re-hear his
praises, but wherever he went he never tired
of insisting upon the fact that it was in his
person that the nation was honouring the
brave men whose enthusiastic support had
made his successes possible.

On February 14, 1881, a couple of meetings

were called to do honour to the gallant leader, which call for special mention as central examples of what went on all over the country wherever Sir Frederick Roberts appeared. These two meetings were both of them held in the City of London ; one was held during the afternoon, when the Corporation presented the distinguished soldier with the freedom of the City and also with a magnificent sword of honour, "in recognition of his valuable services in Afghanistan, where, supported by brave soldiers, he so well and nobly upheld the prestige and reputation of the British army." The brilliant ceremonial took place in the library at Guildhall, and the company included the ex-Viceroy of India, Lord Lytton. The City Chamberlain having addressed the returned Commander in terms that, however flattering, were by no means undeserved, General Roberts replied as follows :—"Believe me that I use language in no conventional manner when I say that I cannot in adequate terms express my sense of the great honour which has this day been awarded to me. Excepting the distinctions which our Sovereign has been graciously pleased to bestow on me, none of the generous testimonies which I have received has more deeply stirred my feelings of gratitude. The honours which have been paid to me in this historical hall are considerably enhanced by the very gratifying manner in which you have referred first to the memory of my honoured father, whose counsels and examples have stimulated my exertions in the path of duty; then to the circumstances of my earlier career; and, lastly, to the services which in recent years I have been enabled to render to my Queen and country. In the honourable grant of the freedom of this City and of a sword of honour to a soldier like myself, I recognise, not only the approval of the most important municipal corporation in these realms, but also your appreciation of the fact that arms are necessary to the protection of commerce and to the secure enjoyment of peace. When I call to mind the list of illustrious commanders on whom this much-coveted distinction has from time to time been bestowed, I cannot but feel that the addition of my name to the list is owing rather to your

favour than to my own merit. Permit me to
accept the honour as paid, not to myself alone,
but also to the able officers and to the brave
and enduring troops who served under my
directions, and whom I am so proud to repre-
sent. Your Chamberlain has paid me and the
force which I commanded, a high compliment
indeed in comparing our march from Kabul to
Kandahar with the famous ' retreat of the ten
thousand' from the plains of Babylon to the
shores of the Euxine. To a certain extent,
we may, perhaps, be permitted to accept this
comparison. Both operations were carried
out amidst numerous enemies and through
difficult countries, and in both cases the object
in view was successfully attained. Honour is
the proper reward of a soldier's services, and
'dangers,' according to no mean authority,
' ask to be paid in pleasure.' I need not assure
you of the pleasure with which I have this
day received the highest tokens of your appro-
bation."

It is, of course, as I have suggested,
impossible to refer to the many speeches
delivered by the General during these

months, when he was being called upon
and over again to respond to the toa
his health and to acknowledge the hoi
thrust upon him by an admiring nation.
two speeches delivered on this February
must be taken as representative of all,
they certainly illustrate the fact which, a
Duke of Cambridge, the then Command(
Chief said, had struck him, that whei
General Roberts was called upon to spe(
never forgot those who had served under

In the evening of the day named a
attended banquet was given to the he
the hour at the Mansion House, and
toast of Sir Frederick's health having
proposed, the great soldier rose and deli)
a long speech full of interest not only t
following his life-story, but also to all
cerned in the welfare of the British a
It is not possible to quote that s{
here at length (it would occupy some fi
pages of this book), but a few of the
notable passages may well be given, as l
among the earliest public utterances oi
brave soldier since he had attained t(

proud position. After acknowledging the compliment which had been paid to him, Sir Frederick Roberts went on to say: "I have so often of late borne testimony to the admirable work which the troops under my command performed in Afghanistan, that I think that it is quite unnecessary to dwell to-night on this, to me, most congenial subject. But on such an occasion as the present, when the services of those troops have been so signally recognised in my person, I think I shall best show my gratitude by giving to this illustrious and most representative assembly the result of my experience as a soldier, who has had opportunities, in more than one campaign, of testing the merits of our past and present systems of army organisation. . . . I am actuated simply by a sincere and honest desire to place my countrymen in possession of the truth about their army, and to do what I can for the army which has done so much for me. I would ask you . . . to remember two essential points about our army. First, that it is England's boast that her army is a volunteer one. Next, that the objects for

which it is maintained are widely different
from the conditions and objects which govern
the requirements of a Continental army. I
understand by a volunteer army *versus* one
raised by conscription that the soldiers belonging to it should, so far as the exigencies
of the service will admit, be treated as volun-
teers throughout their whole career." Sir
Frederick then went on to insist that a recruit
should be permitted to join the particular
regiment for which he had a predilection,
and continued: "Every soldier experienced in
war will tell you that we should do all in our
power to uphold the regimental system, and
to foster and encourage that sensitive plant,
esprit de corps, which, like other sentiments
having their roots in our common nature,
plays as large and influential a part in life
as the dictates of reason itself. . . . We must
never forget that our army is a small one,
almost absurdly small, to meet the many
demands made upon it. Above all things,
then, it is necessary that the spirit and tone
of that army should compensate for its numerical weakness. . . . What is it that has

enabled a comparatively small number of British troops over and over again to face tremendous odds and win battles against vastly superior numbers ? The glorious annals of our regiments give the answer— Discipline, *esprit de corps*, and power of endurance — the three essentials which are absolutely wanting in the young soldier. Discipline enables a man to obey his leaders implicitly, and to rely as implicitly on his comrades, but it cannot be instilled into a young soldier in a few months, and the more short-service men there are in a regiment the longer the process takes. *Esprit de corps* is, as I have said on a former occasion, the backbone of the British army. It is this feeling which teaches our soldiers to take an interest in the traditions of their regiment, and consequently to take pride in helping to keep up its good name. It must be remembered that fighting is not the only demand made upon our soldiers. It is, of course, the main object to be kept in view in any system of training, but all, especially British soldiers, must possess great powers of endurance.

Without them they are really worth nothing. What is it which causes a long casualty roll during a campaign? Not the losses in battle, but the steady, never-ceasing disease brought about by insufficient and badly-cooked food, hard work, night duties, and by exposure to extremes of heat and cold. Against such trials only the strongest can bear up, and unless our regiments are composed of men full-grown and of prime stamina, our armies, in point of numbers weak enough at the best for the work they have to do, must dwindle away very rapidly when they take the field." Sir Frederick Roberts then went on to refer to his experiences with the British troops who were with him during the Kuram Expedition and during his magnificent march, and to plead strongly against the adoption of a " short service " and " reserve " system. "Depend upon it," he went on to say, " the more men and the fewer boys there are in our army the more efficient will our regiments be; and the more the feeling of *esprit de corps* is encouraged the better will duty be carried on. Soldiers have hearts and imaginations like other men. Therefore it is that regiments are proud of their traditions. Therefore it is that the men are proud of a regiment that has made a conspicuous name, and look forward to adding to its reputation. This is *esprit de corps.* . . . With such interests at stake it is surely worth your while to maintain an army on whose services you can always depend. A wealthy and defenceless country is merely a temptation to the cupidity of other nations. But setting all this aside, on the score of economy alone it is of the first importance that our soldiers should be healthy and strong enough to bear the strain of foreign service. . . . While giving my experience of British soldiers, it may, perhaps, be expected of me to say something of her Majesty's native soldiers, with whom I have had so much to do, and of whose many valuable qualities I can speak with some authority. During the war in Afghanistan I had the honour to command troops belonging to the three Presidencies, and I can bear testimony to the loyalty, devotion, and endurance of all, whether they came from Bengal, Madras, or

Bombay. From the experience I gained, I am satisfied that it only requires a careful study of the peculiarities and requirements of the individuals and the localities from which our recruits are drawn to insure the full development of that material which already possesses such admirable qualities. To my mind it is impossible that any one system should be applied successfully to the organisation of an army whose recruiting ground is an empire as large as that of India, and whose units comprise so many different elements. . . . The question of our Indian army, though surrounded by difficulties, is one that must be faced, and I am glad to think that the authorities are alive to the importance of the task they have before them. . . . It has long been in my heart to say to my countrymen what I have said to-night. These are trying times— times in which it behoves every Englishman to think of what is best for the country and the State. We have enemies without and within, and we must not hope to maintain the place we hold in the world unless we are prepared to maintain it alike by the wisdom of our counsels and by the strength and valour of our arms. At such a time it were little less than treason to know, or to believe, that there was a flaw in our armour and not to call attention clearly and earnestly to the fact. This must be my apology. I have spoken warmly and strongly, because, had I not seized this great opportunity to do so, I feel that I should have failed in my duty, not only to the noble service to which I have the great privilege to belong, but also to my country and my Queen."

This speech created a good deal of discussion at the time, and is well worth recalling at the present moment, when the results of the "new system" are being tested in warfare.

One other honour accorded to the hero of Kandahar must be mentioned as showing how proud were the Eton schoolboys of that year of the Eton schoolboy of an earlier date who had so well acquitted himself. The boys of his old college had a sword of honour made for Sir Frederick Roberts, and arrangements were being completed for its presentation when circumstances arose which rendered it necessary that the idea of a public presentation should be abandoned and the sword sent to him privately.*

The circumstances were those in connection with the Boer war. On news reaching England of the tragedy of Amajuba Hill and the death of Sir George Colley, General Roberts was appointed Governor of Natal and Commander-in-Chief of the Forces in South Africa. He left England, but arrived at Cape Town to learn that a peace had been hastily arranged, and to receive instructions to limit his stay in South Africa to four-and-twenty hours. General Roberts arrived back in England, from what he has himself described as a "wild-goose chase," on April 19th, the very day on which Benjamin Disraeli, Earl of Beaconsfield, passed away. It is strange that now, nearly twenty years later, the same General—become a Field-Marshal and a peer —should be sent to the same country to carry out another war with the same enemy.

* This sword was exhibited at the Loan Exhibition held to celebrate the four hundred and fiftieth year of Eton's existence.

During May, 1881, the Queen signified to Sir Frederick Roberts her wish that he should sit to Mr. Frank Holl, A.R.A., for a portrait for her Majesty's own possession.

In June General Roberts—described at the time as "the most popular man in England"—was gazetted a G.C.B. and a baronet for his distinguished services in India. In August of the same year he was the guest of the Emperor of Germany during the military manœuvres in Hanover and Schleswig-Holstein. During the autumn he and Lady Roberts, with their two daughters, returned to India (leaving their son at school in England), where General Roberts took up his duties as Commander-in-Chief in Madras, in which position he continued until August, 1885, during which time he was gazetted as Lieutenant-General—which he had held as "local" rank during the Afghan campaign. During his holding of this command Sir Frederick Roberts made his home at Ootacamund, and had a peaceful time, but for a brief period, when in 1885 war with Russia appeared imminent. In August of that year he was

14

appointed Commander-in-Chief in India, in succession to his friend Sir Donald Stewart, and took up the duties in November, after having paid a short visit to England and had a few weeks' tour on the Continent with his family.

As Commander-in-Chief in India, General Roberts had more power in pressing upon the Governments of India and England the needs of the North-Western Frontier—a subject in which he has always taken the liveliest interest. He was able to do much during his seven years' tenure of office as Commander-in-Chief in getting his views put into practical shape, so that the North-Western Frontier was immeasurably strengthened in the event of any attack from that quarter. In the autumn of 1886 the situation of affairs in Burma was such that General Roberts himself proceeded thither, reaching Rangoon on November 9th. He stayed in that country until the following February, by which time it was becoming pacified.

In the first year of the Queen's Jubilee Sir Frederick Roberts was given the Grand Cross of the Indian Empire, but he found, as he has said, more gratification in the acceptance of an idea of his own for the amelioration of the condition of the troops in India. To use his own words : " What I valued still more was the acceptance by the Government of India of my strong recommendation for the establishment of a club or institute in every British regiment and battery in India. In urging that this measure should be favourably considered, I had said that the British army in India could have no better or more generally beneficial memorial of the Queen's Jubilee than the abolition of that relic of barbarism, the canteen, and its supersession by an institute in which the soldier would have under the same roof a reading-room, recreation-room, and a decently-managed refreshment-room."

The years passed round in performing the duties of this high post, in maturing plans for the defence of the Indian Empire in case of need, and also, as we see by the passage quoted above, in thoughtful consideration for the improvement of the condition of the soldiers on whom that defence depends. At the be-

ginning of 1890 Sir Frederick Roberts was for
the third time offered a high appointment on
the Staff at home, and on this occasion had
accepted it, when a telegram was sent asking
him to retain instead for another two years
the chief command in India. In November,
1890, he was gazetted a full general. It was
1892 before Lord Roberts' long and useful
term of service in India came to an end, and
even then he was asked to still further extend
his period as Commander-in-Chief. At the
beginning of that year the distinguished soldier
was raised to the peerage as Baron Roberts of
Kandahar and Waterford.

In the early part of 1893 Lord Roberts'
"forty-one years in India" were brought to
an end, and he received ovations on all hands
as the time drew near for his departure from
the country in which he was born, in which
he had passed the greater part of his life, and
for which he had performed such sterling
services. He finally left India in April, 1893.

CHAPTER XII

TWO years after his return from India
Lord Roberts was promoted to the rank
of a Field-Marshal—he has the distinction
of being the only one of the eight Field-
Marshals who is the wearer of the Victoria
Cross—and in the autumn of the same year
(1895) he was appointed to the command of
the forces in Ireland. In 1895, too, he first
joined the ranks of the authors with a small
volume on "The Rise of Wellington"—a
book that has much in it of interest to the
student of Lord Roberts' own career. Only
two points from it must detain us here. One
is a brief passage on the all-important question

of military transport, which runs as follows:
"Soldiers, even of the best quality, well
drilled, disciplined, and equipped, cannot hope
to be successful unless proper arrangements
are made for their supply and transport."
The second passage, of especial significance,
coming from a writer with such an unique
knowledge of his subject as Lord Roberts, is
peculiarly interesting: "Another point de-
serving of notice is Wellington's correct
appreciation of our position as an alien Power
controlling a vast heterogeneous Oriental
population. He pointed out, in words as true
now as when they were written, that the
Government of India depends for its stability
on the sword, and that as our responsibility
becomes greater with the extension of our
territory, the cost of the army must pro-
portionately increase."

Writing on New Year's Day, 1898, Lord
Roberts touched once more upon the dangers
menacing the North-Western Frontier of
India: "As one who firmly believes in the
wisdom of Sir Henry Rawlinson's words of
warning, I would venture to express an earnest

hope that they will receive more attention than they have hitherto met with. The subject, which that experienced soldier dealt with so wisely and so fearlessly, is of the most supreme importance to our future in India. The necessity for considering what the real frontier of India is, and how that frontier is to be secured, has forced itself to notice in an unexpected manner during the last few months; and it must have brought home to the most careless observer of Indian frontier politics what an important factor the border tribes are in the question of the defence of the North-West Frontier of our great Indian Empire, and with what enormous difficulties the solution of this most intricate problem is attended." *

Writing towards the close of the same year, Lord Roberts laid stress upon the value of railways in modern warfare, and after citing the then recent Sudan campaign, added: " Again, it is not too much to say that the existence of railways on the North-West

* Introduction to " Memoir of Sir Henry C. Rawlinson."

Frontier of India from Nowshera to Malakand, from Kohat to the Kuram Valley, and from Peshawar round or through the Khyber Pass, would, in all probability, have prevented the late serious rising of the tribesmen, and their construction now would tend more than anything else to ensure their permanent pacification." *

In 1897 General Roberts published " Forty-one Years in India "—a work that deserves to make his name rank as high among auto-biographers as his famous march will make him conspicuous on the page of military history. The book stands alone for its combination of autobiography and history, and is a really remarkable literary performance of which many writers might be proud who had devoted their years as sedulously to culti-vating their profession as Lord Roberts has devoted himself to his. Seeing that in about four years the book has passed through thirty editions, it would appear to enjoy something of the wide popularity which it certainly deserves.

* Introduction to " From Cromwell to Wellington."

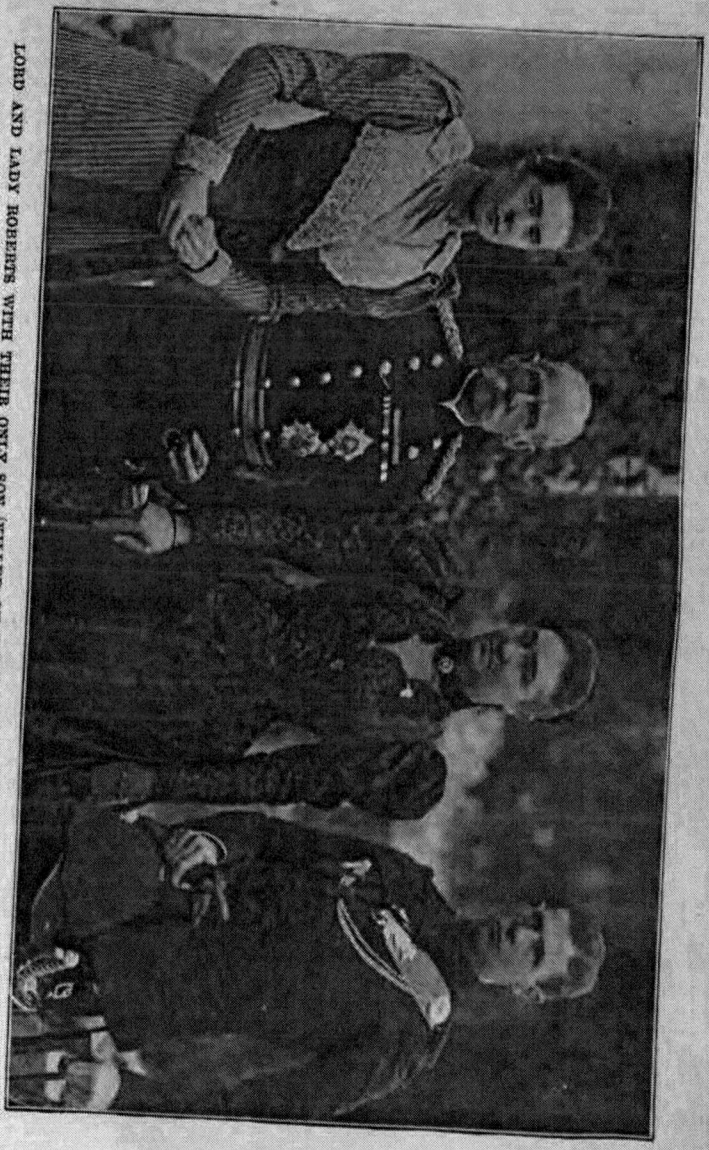

LORD AND LADY ROBERTS WITH THEIR ONLY SON (KILLED ON THE TUGELA) AND ONE OF THEIR DAUGHTERS.

After rather more than a couple of years as Commander of the Forces in Ireland, Lord Roberts has once more been called upon to take command of a large army engaged in a desperate war. In October, 1899, the Transvaal Republic (joined by the neighbouring Republic, the Orange Free State), declared war against Great Britain, and forthwith invaded British colonies in South Africa. Forces were sent out under the chief command of Sir Redvers Buller. The campaign proceeded slowly, and then in December it was found that Natal alone was likely to need all Buller's attention, and that a much larger army was required; and therefore, on December 16th, Lord Roberts was summoned from Dublin to consult with the Government on the serious situation caused by the defeat of General Buller's forces at Colenso. He was offered, and accepted, the supreme command in South Africa, and sailed from Southampton on the following Saturday, December 23rd. What added a poignant pathos to the new appointment was the fact that Lord Roberts' only son was severely wounded in an heroic effort to save the guns at the battle of Colenso, and died on the very day of the appointment. The worthy son of a brave father, Lieutenant F. H. S. Roberts' action was such, that though he has not lived to wear it, he was awarded that most enviable of a soldier's decorations, the Victoria Cross. It is probably an unique instance of a father and son both earning this coveted recognition of personal valour.

Associated with Lord Roberts, as Chief of his Staff, was Lord Kitchener, the victor of Omdurman, to whom is owing the final pacification of the Sudan; and the arrival of the two distinguished soldiers at Cape Town was eagerly anticipated by a public anxious to learn that the tide of events was turning in favour of the British army.

Lord Roberts' departure from England was the occasion for a great display of popular enthusiasm and sympathy for the veteran, who, at the age of sixty-seven, was setting out to undertake the command during what it was fully realised must be a long and serious struggle, and was doing so at a time when suffering from the immeasurable sorrow of the loss of his only son.

Before his departure Lord Roberts sent a "message" to the American and Canadian peoples, which is worth repeating, for its ready appreciation of Colonial loyalty, and for its indignant repelling of certain slanders which had been repeated concerning some of the Irish regiments :—

"Circumstances naturally forbid my speaking about the campaign ahead of me, except to say that I have entire confidence in the British soldier, and that I believe the traditions of our army will be upheld in South Africa. For the friendly interest and sympathy exhibited by many Americans I am deeply grateful. I feel sure that the justice of our cause merits this. Though we be at war, I can safely say that no unnecessary harshness and no acts of inhumanity will mar the fair name of this branch of the Anglo-Saxon race. I cannot too warmly express my admiration of the spirit which prevails in our Colonies. The action of Canada will always be a glorious page in the history of the sons of the Empire. I look for great things from the men she has sent, and is sending, to the front. Reports which indicate that disloyalty exists among Irish regiments are absolutely untrue. In the hour of danger my country-men have ever been among the first to lay down their lives for their Queen and country, and whether it be against Boer or any other nationality, the Irish soldier will be found loyal to his Queen and brave in battle."

Field-Marshal Lord Roberts has had a long and brilliant military career; he has served in many capacities on the Staff and in the field, and is probably to-day our greatest living soldier, and the whole nation is eagerly following the daily story of his work in South Africa, where he finds himself at the head of a larger British army than has ever before been engaged in one of the most difficult wars of our time. That the success which has hitherto been his may attend his present efforts is the devout wish in many thousands of homes in great Britain and the Colonies.

In taking leave of our subject, having briefly followed the story of his career, it is in-teresting to recall Lord Roberts' own words on the qualities necessary to the making of a successful general, written after reading studies of the lives of twelve great military leaders—qualities which this short sketch of his biography shows him to be in possession of himself: " The qualities which distinguish a successful general are practically identical with those which lead to advancement in any other branch of life. In addition to military knowledge and experience, there must be good judgment, sound common sense, tenacity of purpose, quickness of perception, promptitude of decision, and, above all, an infinite capacity for taking pains. No details, however trivial, which can add to the comfort and welfare of the troops, or increase their fighting efficiency, can be neglected without risk of failure. The officer who is fortunate enough to be entrusted with a command in the field should be prepared at all points, and ready to face all contingencies. He should follow Cæsar's example, of whom Lucan wrote: '*Nil actum reputans, dum quid superesset agendum.*' " *

* Introduction to " From Cromwell to Wellington."

UNWIN BROTHERS, THE GRESHAM PRESS, WOKING AND LONDON.

CPSIA information can be obtained at www.ICGtesting.com
Printed in the USA
LVOW131305100513

333216LV00004B/53/A